Helen Stringer

Edited by Sarah Ell

PIONEER WOMEN

PHOTOGRAPH CREDITS: Cover: see p. 75. Back cover images from top: see p. 56; see p. 90; Woman sitting on a hill overlooking a valley, c.1880, O.042376, Museum of New Zealand Te Papa Tongarewa; A woman crossing a log bridge that traverses a small gully, 1880s, A-181-002, Alexander Turnbull Library, Wellington, New Zealand; see p. 85. Title page: Woodland vista, Gift of G.L. Adkin family estate, 1964, MA_I426923, Museum of New Zealand Te Papa Tongarewa. P. 3 Detail from lace square, MA_I140412, Museum of New Zealand Te Papa Tongarewa. P. 4, see pp. 2–3. Pp. 6–7 The full-rigged ship *Caribou* at Taieri Head off the Otago Coast, c.1867, MA_I081444, Museum of New Zealand Te Papa Tongarewa. Pp. 22–23 Family group, c.1890s, Gift of the Guard family, 1993, O.003692, Museum of New Zealand Te Papa Tongarewa. Pp. 44–45: Oldhams Creek, Nelson, O.036725, Museum of New Zealand Te Papa Tongarewa. Pp. 60–61 The last bush fire on the South Block 20-2-05, Gift of G.L. Adkin family estate, 1964, A.005847, Museum of New Zealand Te Papa Tongarewa. Pp. 80–81 Angela Jacob washing outdoors, Manawatu, O.030734, Museum of New Zealand Te Papa Tongarewa. Pixabay: pp. 9, 27, 42, 43, 91. Courtesy Mangawhai Museum: p. 19 Baby's dress, Ref. 15-64; p. 28 Copper, Ref. 16-198; p. 31 Hand corn husker, Ref: 637; p. 34 Camp oven, Ref. 34; p. 36 Milking stool, Ref. 17-82; p. 41 Butter pats, Ref. 73; p. 57 Apron, Ref. 955; p. 84 Food strainer, Ref. 180. Courtesy Arthur Elworthy: p. 54. Courtesy Sarah Elworthy: p. 64.

Published by Oratia Books, Oratia Media Ltd,
783 West Coast Road, Oratia, Auckland 0604, New Zealand
(www.oratia.co.nz)

Copyright © Bush Press Communications and Sarah Ell
Copyright © 2019 Oratia Books (published work)

The copyright holders assert their moral rights in the work.

This book is copyright. Except for the purposes of fair reviewing, no part of this publication may be reproduced or transmitted in any form or by any means, whether electronic, digital or mechanical, including photocopying, recording, any digital or computerised format, or any information storage and retrieval system, including by any means via the Internet, without permission in writing from the publisher. Infringers of copyright render themselves liable to prosecution.

ISBN 978-0-947506-59-9

Managing editor: Carolyn Lagahetau
Designer: Sarah Elworthy

Contestable Fund Grant recipient 2017

First published 2019
Printed in China

CONTENTS

Introduction 4

THE VOYAGE OUT
'Hopeful' 8
Charlotte Godley 11
Jane Findlayson 16

A NEW LIFE
Harriet Langford 24
Sarah Higgins 29
Martha Adams 33
Alicia Wilhemina Chitty 39

ADVENTURES AND EXPLORATIONS
Sarah Mathew 46
Caroline Chevalier 50
Eleanor Adams 55

WAR AND DISASTER
Elizabeth Holman 62
Rhoda Coote 67
Lady Mary Anne Barker 71
Amy Paterson 76

WOMEN AT WORK
Jane Maria Richmond 82
Lizzie Heath 86
Margaret Fidler 91
Ellen Wilson and other witnesses 94

Acknowledgements and sources 99
Index 100

INTRODUCTION

The pioneer women in this book tell their own stories. Their tales are culled from old books and manuscripts. The idea behind the selection is to show the range and variety of pioneer experience and give some idea of the adventurous spirit that was required.

The common thread is that of women in an unfamiliar country coming to terms with new circumstances and generally making another life. There is high adventure, such as crossing a mountain range or surviving a volcanic eruption. There is also adventure of a more domestic kind, adventures of the mind and spirit, such as in the realisation that the English past is no longer helpful, and that settlers who wish to succeed need a new way. From these experiences comes a picture of the kind of spirit required of the first European settlers and how they began to forge the traditions that we value as New Zealanders today.

If it were not for the wealth of personal material lodged by New Zealand families in institutions such as the Alexander Turnbull Library in Wellington, much of New Zealand's heritage might have remained only in official versions, surviving only as government records, or as second-hand reports and analysis by academics. Here, women speak for themselves, in ways that might seem hard-headed or even hard-hearted to modern readers. The quality of nineteenth century life on the frontiers of New Zealand demanded an unsentimental outlook among the successful pioneers, whatever romantic values modern day readers might ascribe to the Victorians.

Although this book does not record the voices of Maori women, it is fully acknowledged that they were as much pioneers in maintaining, creating and building a lifestyle and culture as their counterparts who arrived from overseas.

These are the stories of pioneer women who have come to New Zealand from countries far away, most commonly England. The women tell brave, enterprising and inspiring stories, yet they are also often disturbing and discomfiting. They speak directly from the past. Their words are printed largely to enjoy but there are echoes along the way that may also challenge the way we think today.

A NOTE ON THE EDITING

Much of the text reproduced here has been taken directly from transcripts of pioneer diaries, letters and reminiscences. Where spelling has been distractingly erratic or misleading corrections have been made. The syle of expression has been left in its original form, without benefit of editing for clarity. Consequently, the text sometimes reflects idiosyncractic fashion.

Generally, Maori words have been allowed to stand in their contemporary form but with the occasional addition of modern placenames and spellings in parenthesis where this helps to place the story less ambiguously.

Distances and areas are given in their original Imperial form, with a mile equal to 1.6 km and an acre being 0.4 of a hectare.

THE VOYAGE OUT

'HOPEFUL'
A FIT PERSON TO EMIGRATE

'Disappointed' might have been a better nom-de-plume than 'Hopeful' for a young Englishwoman identified only as Maggie who emigrated to Christchurch in 1885. Her letters to her brother were published in 1887 under the title of Taken In, '... because there is a great deal of false information afloat respecting Colonial facts ...'

In this piece she summarises the qualities she thinks an emigrant requires to live in the new colony.

Dear Brother,

In this letter I will try and write a little on the classes who may venture out and those who should not, and this information I have gathered from most careful investigation of these matters on my own part, also from statistics and from general enquiry.

1. *The class who may venture to come out*

The class who may venture to come out should be those of good and strong constitution and thoroughly prepared to *rough it*! Also men of speculative tendencies, good business habits, and sufficient money to start them in some business or mercantile speculation. For instance, labourers and country mechanics such as wheelwrights, blacksmiths, harness-makers, rough carpenters, and a generally hard-working class, and those habituated to work for generations have, perhaps a better chance here than at home, as wages are better than in the old country, and food is cheap; but for the town artisan and superior mechanic there is very little demand …

2. The class who should never venture to come out
Well-to-do ladies and gentlemen, who have been well brought up, as also have their families for generations before them — this class is *utterly useless* in the colonies and constantly has to endure *great* hardships.

Again, ladies and gentlemen in reduced circumstances rarely succeed in the Colonies; their small income would go twice as far and give them treble the comforts at home; 30s a week here would be no more than £1 a week at home, and as I have explained before, the price of every thing except food, is generally far higher. There is another class who would not improve their condition here, namely, that of upper servants of well-to-do families — these feel sadly disappointed at their prospects on arrival. …

As I have said before, New Zealand has more than enough to do in finding employment for the numerous Colonial girls who abound in town and country. As to marriage — well that word will ever have an intense

> **"Taken In."**
> This volume is composed of a series of letters by a young lady to her brother in Canada, giving a glimpse of New Zealand life as seen by her. "Hopeful" (this is the *nom de plume* adopted by the writer) may have written according to her own experience, but we ('European Mail') doubt many of her statements, and think she has looked with jaundiced eyes on the many advantages to be gained by settlers of both sexes in our colonies generally, but especially New Zealand. In a preface to the work she counts herself as one of those "misguided and foolish people" who believe in "the sunny south as the land of promise, the land of plenty, and the land of hope." She appeared to think that she had only to go to New Zealand, and her fortune was made; that on landing her services would be in demand, and at her own price. She appears to have had a sad awakening, however, and learnt all in good time that there was little opening for educated and delicately-nurtured young ladies, that class—like the clerk and the ne'er-do-well—being a drug in the market. "Hopeful" appears to have been a dreamer, and sees nothing good in colonial life. According to her "there is not the same check and restraint on people out here, and especially on the rising youth, as at Home. . . . The youth of both sexes have far too much run of the streets, and the 'larrikin,' as the rising young man is called, is often a mischevious specimen of later manhood, and his street liberty degenerates into vice.

An excerpt of a review of Hopeful's publication.

Papers Past, National Library of New Zealand. *Evening Star*, Issue 7502, 21 April 1888, Supplement

What's a wheel-wright?
A craftsperson who builds or repairs wooden wheels.

fascination to the female mind — and so one is not so surprised to find, after reading the glowing accounts given of the country (generally by those who are interested in giving these accounts), that many females are brought out (the country is deluged with them) who discover, poor things, to their chagrin on arrival, that they have no chance of either honourable work or the much wished for husband. Many respectably, and even well educated and well brought-up girls and women, have come out in this way, to their cost, and find themselves in a sorry plight; 'they cannot dig, to beg they are ashamed,' so they go down, *down*, and the history of many, is sad indeed.

3. *The characters and constitutions that should come out*
The constitutions well suited for Colonial life, are those that are *very strong*, and that can live and thrive on those things that are cheap. The characters, who can drive a hard bargain. Those who love money-grubbing to the depth of their souls, and care not what hardness or trouble they go through to attain this much wished for goal, and those who have little softness or refinement in their nature, will get on well.

4. *The characters that should not come out*
The characters not suited for Colonial life are those endued with sympathetic, imaginative, poetic and refined tastes, also those with affectionate and appreciative natures. The more developed these qualities are in any individual who comes out, the more he will suffer; the more painful will be the terrible roughness of Colonial life to such a soul, and the more sadly will such a one pine for home and the genial companionships of other days.

CHARLOTTE GODLEY
THE VOYAGE OUT

Charlotte Godley (née Wynne) came to New Zealand with her husband John Robert Godley, Chief Agent of the Canterbury Association, organisers of the New Zealand Company settlement on the Canterbury Plains. With a two-year-old son, John Arthur (known as Arthur), they sailed from Plymouth in December 1849 aboard the Lady Nugent.

Charlotte first stepped on New Zealand soil in Dunedin, and had an early chance to observe the manners of the Scottish settlement at Dunedin, founded by the Otago Association in 1848. The Godleys then spent six months in Wellington before returning to Canterbury to await the arrival of the First Four ships in December 1850.

January 7th, 1850
Latitude 7°9'. Thermometer 78°.

My Dear Mother,
… We left Antonie, as you know, after luncheon on Wednesday, December 12th, and got on board just before dark, and remained that night in Plymouth Sound. We sailed the next morning at about 11, and in six hours the wind came dead against us, and on the next Tuesday morning we were still not 30 miles from Plymouth, and the wretchedness of those days is not a thing to be lightly spoken of. Arthur, Powles and I were all [sea sick] at once, and I think I

was the least ill of the three, for though Arthur was not so bad at the time and slept a good deal, he has not recovered the effects of it still, and looks so thin and wretched, though he is certainly better this last week. But he feels the motion as much as I do, and that is whenever it is the least rough.

My husband was very sick for two days, but his throat got perfectly well from the moment he came on board for a fortnight; now it is rather troublesome again, for we have had some hot, heavy weather, and he is not the better for it. Our stern cabin is a great comfort in this weather, as it is always airy; at first it was like sitting with the window open and no fire, and that is pretty cold at sea in December, but it will be a great thing for us now.

Please tell Aunt Jane how very acceptable the cloak was, although I cannot think of it with any coolness to-day, within eight degrees of the Line. We have had some lovely sunrises and the stars are very beautiful, but I am sorry to say we have lost the Great Bear now, which seems quite a part of home. No sharks yet, but the lines are out for them to-day. Arthur had a flying fish for his dinner on Saturday, to his great delight. It flew on to the deck, poor little thing, and the Captain made him a present of it. We have had quantities flying about for the last three days and they are beautiful little creatures, but quite small, only about eight inches long. We have seen a few of Mother Carey's chickens, too, and some shoals of porpoises. But the prettiest thing is to sit on the deck at night quite at the stern and watch the track of the vessel; last night it was like three wreaths of pale green smoke (one from each side and one from the rudder) studded with showers of bright stars. The Captain says there will be more of it, too, soon. We like him very much; he is extremely civil to us and almost too good-natured to everyone in the ship.

> **What are Mother Carey's chickens?**
>
> Mother Carey's chickens is an alternative name for seabirds of the storm petrel family.

Charlotte Godley, 1877.

19XX.2.965, etching by W.E. Miller, 1877. Cantebury Museum

January 9th

The breeze is over. We were woke before four on the morning after I wrote last by a thunderstorm and a squall, and then the wind went all round the compass and disappeared. The lightning was very vivid and such rain, but the rudder and its chains rattled so at our heads that we could hardly hear the thunder, and then we had a day's rolling in heavy swell and no wind, which brought us headaches, and a little shark. I have seen dog-fish quite as large, so that I was not much excited, but this morning we had a big one on our hook several times, but not caught, and two smaller ones, not four feet long, caught.

This is a beautiful, hot day, but still a little breeze, thermometer about 81, by the aneroid Tom gave my husband, latitude 5°13' at noon, and it has been really beautiful, all the day, to see the sharks playing about, with the pilot fishes all around them, down in the deep blue water under our stern windows. Arthur in delight, as you may suppose, and we each tasted a bit of one broiled, and very nasty we thought it. Mr. Tollemache took up one head after it had been off ten minutes and tried to frighten one of the children with it, but instead he got a good bite on his own thumb to the great amusement of the spectators ...

January 12th
We have now come up again with the *Maid* [*of the Mill,* a ship going towards Buenos Aires], and now in a calm, so my letter had better go, and I shall begin another, in case of meeting still with one homeward bound. Arthur is much better, and hopping about in only a shirt and white pinafore. It is piping hot, and now Goodbye. Yours ever, with much love to everyone.

> *The* Lady Nugent *was 112 days at sea from Plymouth to her first landfall at Port Chalmers, Otago Harbour. They sight the Cape of Good Hope but do not touch land, sweeping along the Roaring Forties, to approach New Zealand from the south of Stewart Island. There, in the vicinity of the Snares Islands, they are again swept up by a storm.*

Lady Nugent, *March 23rd*
IN SIGHT OF NEW ZEALAND! But we have now had a real storm, and I should be very glad indeed to think that I should never see another. It began on Sunday the 17th, and in the afternoon we had our dead lights put in for the first time and we are still in darkness. Monday was rough, but nothing wonderful, and the two next days the same; on Thursday the wind blew very hard, and, high as we are out of the water, we were inundated even in the cuddy, great waves splashing quite over the side of the ship; and the land being due next day (Friday) the Captain got rather anxious. We had a quiet night, and some sleep, and then another sudden fall of the barometer promised another gale of wind which accordingly began after breakfast, and very beautiful the sea was when I went up about noon, to see it. The spray was blown from

the top of each wave till the whole sea looked like a snow storm, white with foam. We must then have been within 100 miles of land, but it was very thick; and as we had not seen land, to prove the chronometers, for three months, it was enough to put the Captain rather in a fidget; especially as the gale increased, and the barometer was falling rapidly. There is a reef called the Snares about 40 miles south of Stewart Island, and our course ran between the two. We would have hove to, but did not dare, there was such a heavy sea on, for fear of the decks being swept, as she came round; so there was nothing for it but to go on running, which we accordingly did. ... We carried a closereefed foresail and maintopsail all night, expecting them to go every minute, but they held on, and consequently so did the ship, and we made little or no leeway. About 12, the wind moderated again to a whole gale; the glass began to rise as soon as the hurricane came on, and though there were some tremendous squalls until 4.30, we felt the worst of the danger was over. At daylight the Captain, calculating that he had well weathered the Cape, hauled up to the northward; there was a rumour of land at 6.30, but it died away again, and at 8 o'clock the mist cleared off a little, and there was land sure enough on the larboard bow. ...

A £1 note from the 1850s, Otago Banking Company. In today's money this would be worth approximately $120. Reserve Bank of New Zealand Museum

In the night we lay to, and then drifted too far to the northward; the breeze freshened, and kept us beating about all Sunday the 23rd, and on Monday we had another gale, almost if not quite as bad as the Friday before, only then we knew where we were. Tuesday, we were all up early and in great spirits, with a fair wind blowing straight into the [Otago] harbour, and at noon in we came, at a great pace. The entrance is very narrow as there are sand banks, covered at high water, which run nearly across the Bay. But it is so beautiful. It is eight miles from the point up to Port Chalmers, which is a little bay in the harbour, and there *Lady Nugent* is now lying, in a perfect nest of beauty, and as snug as a ship can be.

JANE FINDLAYSON
MEASLES AND MADNESS

Young single women such as Jane Findlayson were among one of the most sought-after groups of emigrants to New Zealand in the nineteenth century. Single women were much in demand in the new colony, both as wives and domestic servants, and were encouraged to travel out with family members or their employers. Those behind the colonisation of New Zealand saw women as being doubly useful to the growing colony: not only would the eventual birth of their children supply the new country with further population and labour force, but the women themselves would also act as a 'civilising influence' on their countrymen.

Jane and her friend Agnes left the Scottish port of Greenock, on the River Clyde near Glasgow, in September 1876, on the ship Oamaru *bound for the Otago Association settlement of Dunedin.*

16th [October, 1877]

We could not get on deck this morning it being very wet, [so we were] glad when it faired as it was nearly suffocation down below. We have often heard of Equatorial heat but this is it in reality. We wear nothing but our dress and shoes on our hard feet, some go without shoes but that we can't manage. There is a young Irish girl went wrong in her mind beside us, we did not get any sleep for four nights she talked on, so we complained to the doctor and she has tonight been taken to hospital. We are all sorry for her brother who is waiting on her till the Doctor arranges other plans for her …

20th
This is another hot day we are in prospects of crossing the line in a few days. The girl who went wrong in her mind is getting worse. She is harmless as yet. She has spoken and sung continually for nearly a week. She does not know any of us now, her eyes are quite vacant. The sailors had a performance tonight, they threw their 'dead horse' into the sea. It is an affair they get up at the end of the first month, we were up on the poop and saw the whole affair on the main deck below. (145 miles)

23rd
We passed a restless night owing to Lizzie, she is getting fractious now and tries to belt anyone who goes near her, she is quite near us here and keeps pelting at the door with her hands and feet, she is worn to a shadow and eats nothing scarcely. … We got damped all of a sudden with the news of the death of a child aged one year and eight months, the funeral is to be tomorrow morning at half past 7.

24th
We were all up and dressed by 7 o'clock and went on deck where the little child was laid out sewed in canvas and covered with the ship's flag, the service was read and at the words 'I commit this body to the deep' it was put through the porthole and with a great splash in the water it was all over, it was very solemn and we did not

> **The 'dead horse' ceremony**
>
> A ceremony performed on board a ship at the end of the first month at sea. Merchant seamen were often given an 'advance note' equalling a months' pay to enable them to purchase goods before setting sail. Sailors often referred to their first month of work at sea as 'working for a dead horse'. The ceremony would include the dropping of a crude effigy of a horse into the sea.

feel the least appetite for our breakfast. There is to be no fun today owing to the funeral. We crossed the line about 6 o'clock tonight.

25th
This is a lovely morning, we hurried on deck to see two beautiful vessels in sight, they were in full sail and looked fine at a distance. There are lots of preparations going on about the main deck preparing for the afternoon's performance.

About 3 o'clock a procession came on deck consisting of King Neptune, his wife, his Doctor, clerk and barber as well as six black slaves following them. The captain received them graciously and told the King to give him a call again after he had the rest of his business done, so he went on the main deck and shaved all the new hands on board, the purser, cabin boy, (one of the cabin passengers for fun) as well as about a dozen more sailors, bakers, stewards, etc. After being shaved they were plunged into a big tank of water where the slaves were swimming about and ready to give them a proper dunking. It was two hours grand fun and that did not finish the day, the singers' names were taken down for a concert in the evening. I wished Tom had been there as comic songs were scarce and when they were sung were loudly applauded, about eight girls and ten men sang, the songs were enjoyed most were such as 'I'm a Scotchman born' and 'Auld Lang Syne', these put us in mind of home. ... We had a birth on board about 6 o'clock tonight, a young married woman had her first baby (a daughter) both are doing well ...

28th
We are going on nicely but the heat is sickening, we shall be glad when the weather gets a little colder. Lizzie is no better in her mind, she tries all she can to commit suicide and many a fright she gives us. We had another concert tonight it makes the time pass pleasantly, there are some good singers among the young men and very willing they are.

7th [November]
Lizzie has broken up the door of the hospital twice. She is more sensible than she was and when we ask her at the outside of the door how she is, she knows our word fine and answers as sensible enough. She has torn up her bedclothes with her teeth and a dresser of her own she has beside her, they have taken everything out of the room, she lies on boards with a strong quilt over her, we don't know how she lives with so little sleep. (145 miles)

27th
Cold weather again but we are going on nicely, we did not sleep well last night, some way or another we felt in a mood for talking of home, we also have a good company of rats beside us, they run about in dozens, we need to take care and not leave any of our clothes in their way else they would make a gob of them. We had our salt beef today and preserved carrots, the batter we ate but we threw the beef overboard. …

30th
We were sorry to hear of another child's death with measles, we went to the funeral service at 6 o'clock, the mother was pretty brave considering. We hope there will be no more deaths, it puts us all about to hear of it.

3rd [December]
Unfortunately there is a fresh case of measles this morning, there is no doubt now but we will be quarantined, we are going on rapidly and as steady as can be.

4th
This is a very cold day, we expected warm weather 'ere now. Another case of measles into the hospital, the doctor has lots to do with them all.

5th
There was any amount of dancing among the girls today …

6th
Another boy seven years old went in with measles. … A married man has taken a fever of Rheumatism he can't stir himself, it will be a sad landing for his family. A great change has come during the night, we are making slow progress. (206 miles)

7th
We are in hopes to be landed in a week or little more. I am ashamed to tell you that one of our girls was confined of a daughter last night at half past 9, the doctor sent us all off from where he was, our place is sort of two apartments with only a short stair between us so just fancy 28 girls put out of their place, some of them took their beds with them and lay on the floor, we did not do so but on a form, we spent most of the night telling stories and any little bits of fun to amuse ourselves, we got back to our beds about 6 in the morning and stayed till dinner time. … (180 miles)

8th
We got praise from the doctor about having our place so clean, he says the inspectors who come on board are very particular. We feel a change in the weather, we are now corning into the New Zealand climate. Another case of measles and what is worse it's among us, one little girl being between three and four is away to hospital, some of the mothers beside us are in a sad state, it is almost sure to spread, there are 13 children among us. (140 miles)

9th
We were wakened out of our first sleep by a commotion … [a] young infant being found dead beside its mother, it is supposed she had overlaid it. She is a young girl not 19 without much sense, she appeared to be in a sad state about it, poor thing, it's best away it puts us off our sleep for an hour or two. (180 miles)

11th
This is a fine day the heat is up to 62 degrees, everyone is making preparations for landing, the doctor told us this morning we would be in quarantine for a week at least, we hope to get to our destination before New Year. I forgot to say there was a birth yesterday morning in the married quarters (not here) and unfortunately another child died of measles last night, the doctor was driven nearly stupid, an old man took an apoplectic fit but is partly recovered, there is a child bad with typhoid fever so that the trouble is increasing rather than diminishing. We don't eat much now and feel agitated at the thought of going ashore, we are glad that there will be time for a telegram before the New Year. (246 miles)

16th
Thank God we are safely anchored in Port Chalmers but the yellow flag has been hoisted and we are doomed to be quarantined for a week at least. We stay on the ship all night and tomorrow, [then] we go on an island for the purpose where we will have every convenience for getting our things all washed, the married folks are on one end of it and we are on another and what is most laughable is the young men are put on an island opposite us with the water between.

Quarantine Island with the hospital buildings on a knoll, and jetty below.

1/2-003221-G, photographed by David Alexander De Maus, 1880s. Alexander Turnbull Library, Wellington, New Zealand

HARRIET LANGFORD
THE BRITANNIA SETTLERS

Harriet Bates, the daughter of a Birmingham timber merchant, married James Alfred Langford on 31 August 1839. Ten days later they set sail on the barque Aurora, *one of the three initial New Zealand Company immigrant ships. On their departure from England, a site had not been selected for the first settlement, and things had progressed little by the time the ships arrived at Port Nicholson, now Wellington Harbour, in January 1840. Surveyors had arrived to lay out the 'Britannia' settlement just weeks before, and no work had been done on clearing the land or building shelter for the 1000 emigrants who arrived over the next three months.*

The Langfords' first child was born in December, shortly before the couple moved to Auckland. The couple had six sons and five daughters. John died in 1894 and Harriet four years later, aged 80. These reminiscences, held by the Alexander Turnbull Library, were written for her children.

On nearing New Zealand the Captain was uncertain about the port of his destination, so put into Port Hardy [at D'Urville Island in the Marlborough Sounds]. Some of the officers went on shore and on their return shortly afterwards, we left again and proceeded to Port Nicholson (Wellington). On going into the harbour the wind was high, and the anchor being in some way impeded, the second mate went forward to chop away the impediment, which being done, it rushed out with such force that he was severely hurt and was carried into the cabin. It was on the 22nd January 1840 that we arrived at Wellington, or rather it was at Petone where we landed, the site of the township of Wellington not having been settled then. There had been an attempt at putting up some wooden buildings for stores for the New Zealand company, but as yet there was neither roof nor sides, only the frames against which some boards were placed, and we crept under, glad to be away from the ship. Some of the officers coming that way asked if we would not come back to the boat for the present, as a drizzling rain was falling. But I declined, as the air felt so mild I did not fear taking cold. In a few days another vessel arrived and they fired a salute, but in doing so a young man named Burr had his two arms blown off. He was brought into the building to have them amputated.

About this time father joined a staff of

Part of Lambton Harbour in Port Nicholson, showing about a third of the water frontage of the town of Wellington, 1841.

Heaphy, Charles, 1820–1881, OUR Heritage, http://Otago.ourheritage.ac.nz/items/show/5327, Hocken Collections, Uare Taoka o Hākena, University of Otago

Harriet was one of the signatories on the Suffrage Petition to Parliament, which was instrumental in securing voting rights for women in New Zealand.

Archives New Zealand

surveyors under Mr Park, and I decided to go with him up the River Hutt. Four or five others went also, and there was a tent for us to live in. We were there two or three weeks, but the mosquitos bit me terribly that I had not a free place about me. Some of the men set about to build a house for us to live in. One day my husband went with some of the others down to Petone for provisions, and on their return got bewildered in the bush and could not find their way back until the morning.

They had brought muskets back for themselves and the others, with the news that a war had broken out among the natives and therefore we had to be on our guard. A few days after, being Sunday, as we were taking a stroll we found there was a beaten path at the back of our tent, which was not very reassuring, as we knew that it could only be trodden by natives, so that at any moment we might be surprised by a war party. After that, now and then in the day one of the men would come back with a pigeon they had shot for my dinner, or some errand; but afterwards I found that it was only an excuse to see if I was safe and all right.

One morning when the men had left, gone to their work, I heard a terrible crackle, crackle of broken twigs, and I stood watching where the sounds came from (for in the bush sounds seem to be multiplied). But when the cause was revealed, it was Mr Park, armed to the teeth; a pair of pistols in his belt, a tomahawk hanging therefrom, and a sort of dagger besides his gun. He crossed over the fallen tree which served us [for] a bridge, to where I was standing. I asked him if he did not think I had better put the muskets out of sight, in case of the natives coming and taking them, for they were piled outside the tent in military fashion, but he replied 'If you see natives, put yourself out of sight and never mind the muskets.' However the natives did not trouble us.

The next time the men went down, they brought word that a woman who had fallen down one of the hatchways on the ship after I left, had not long to live and no one would attend her. So I at once said that I would go and do what I could. My husband went part of the way with me. I reached the boat during the forenoon and found the woman in a deplorable condition often convulsed, and with few comforts. She died about twelve o'clock that night, leaving a little girl about two years old. I called to her husband, but he gave a sort of grunt and said, 'Poor thing' and I could see him turn himself over and then he said, 'Well, I suppose you don't want me.' I replied, 'I should think I do, I want some clothing for her.' However, there was none to be had in that quarter, but fortunately my own boxes were not far off. Next day I collected what rags were available belonging to

What's a barque?

A barque is a sailing vessel with three or more masts, each with square sails except for that on the aft mast.

the poor woman, and having cleaned them, set about to clothe the poor child, and by the time I had finished, the fatigue added to the rain dripping down on us through the leaky roof, was too much for me and I was very ill. When the Doctor came he said he ought to have been called sooner. However, in a few days I began to mend.

By the time I was well the house was ready for occupation. Mrs Houghton and I got on well together, except sometime when by her thoughtlessness, my coffee pot or saucepan would lose spout or handle as she had no cooking utensils. She was a poor thoughtless young creature.

I ought to have said before that after most of us had left the vessel, a Mrs Sawyer who nursed Mrs Park when her baby was born and afterwards assisted her with the baby, was herself confined. At that time the hatches on the boat were open for the discharge of the luggage, and Mrs Glover hastening past to get something that was wanted, fell down the hatchway, sustaining the injury that caused her death. A few days after her confinement, Mrs Sawyer wanting something, got out of bed to get it herself, caught a cold and died, the two women being buried within a few days of each other.

SARAH HIGGINS
'GETTING ALONG, LITTLE BY LITTLE'

Sarah Sharp was 12 when she emigrated to Nelson with her family. Her mother had died when Sarah was a baby, and her father's second wife had also died a year after their marriage; so Sarah was brought up by her grandparents at Stephen Sharp's home in Kent. Although she attended school long enough to learn to sew and read, she could not write.

Stephen Sharp applied to take his two daughters and three sons to the New Zealand Company settlement of Nelson, but was initially refused because he did not have a wife. Eventually the family left on the Bolton in 1842.

Once in New Zealand, Sarah was responsible for the family's housekeeping, and also went into domestic service. She married Sidney Higgins and settled in Nelson. Sarah died in 1925, aged 94. This account is recorded in a typescript of her reminiscences held by both the Alexander Turnbull and Hocken libraries.

Our next door neighbour had a little baby girl and I used to go and stay with her after the women had been in and attended to the Mother and baby. There were no nurses to be had then so the women helped to nurse one another. I could get anything she wanted and nurse the baby, she was such a pretty little dear. It has happened that baby's oldest son is married to my youngest daughter.

It was a sorry time with the poor woman in their baby troubles,

Sarah Higgins.
34588, Tyree Studio Collection, Nelson Provincial Museum

Passenger list for the *Bolton* included Sarah's family as:

SHARP

Stephen 39
Agricultural Labourer

Susannah 19
Servant

Robert 18
Agricultural Labourer

George 12

Sarah 10

she would be weak for the want of food. I took some of the potatoes up out of the ground that her husband had planted and cooked them for her. Our vegetables had grown and we had a nice lot of parsnips. I used to boil some and take [them] into her, she used to enjoy them.

Then Mr Dupper got over a lot of wheat and let the men have it for work done for him. They began to grow their own and there was no mill to grind it when we had grown it. The company sent out some coffee mills and they fixed them to posts and we would take it in turns to grind our lot then we baked it bran and all.

When the corn was fit to cut we had to use knives, after a while we got some reaphooks, then we could cut it better. That was how we began to get along, little by little. It was very lonely for me to be by myself so much. I used to go to the neighbours to help them and do sewing for the children. I thought I would like to go to a lady's place and learn to do things like they did. I had been to Mrs Otterson's and she seemed a nice lady, she asked me about my home and I told her all about it. She said she would like me to come and live with her and I told her I would like it very much. I told my father but he did not like to let me go. I did not go just then, she sent up three times and asked Mr Jeffries about me. She said that she had taken a fancy to me. Then she sent Mr Fivin with the bullock cart and I went for a month to try it. The work was very hard after having such an easy time at home. Mr Otterson kept nine cows, and there were nine in the family, and a large house. He kept a lot of men to work for him. I asked a neighbour if she would see to father's things and I would pay her a little for it.

They all got very fond of me and I did of them. Mr Jeffries split fencing for Mr Otterson so I often saw him and could hear about my father. I only had 2/- a week and I wanted to learn to milk so that I could milk our own cow when we could get one. I made butter and cheese, learned cooking and baking and housework. I had been there only three months when Mrs Otterson gave me 4/- a week. After a few months she gave me 6/-, then I bought myself some nice things. She told me what was advisable to get. They kept a store for the homestead and I was there 14 months.

Well, then I went home to my father and my boy, for I did have one that came sometimes. He was the same boy that helped the baker make the mud oven to bake the bread, and he was with the men making the road around the beach when I came ashore. He had come in three months before our ship came, and I did not notice him but he did me. When he was with the baker and brought the bread to us he went home and told his mother he had seen the prettiest girl he had ever seen and he would have her for his wife if he could get her, so he never lost sight of me long. ...

I was home once more with my father and the hard times were getting better. My father had bought a cow while I was away so I had a cow to milk. I also took in sewing and had a lot to do. My brother had a dog and ammunition and he used to get a wild pig occasionally and we had a lot of nice vegetables.

When I had been home about a year Sidney wanted to be married but I wanted to wait until I was 21, but he said he could not have much for a home while he had to pay board when he was only getting 2/6 a day. He got my father's consent by promising he would not take me away from home, so then I gave in. He and Mr Jeffries cut the timber and he got Mr Wratt to build it.

It was a nice large room built onto my father's house and took six weeks to build it. We were to be married on the Monday after it was finished. It

The town and part of the harbour of Nelson in 1842, a year after its first foundation.

Saxton, John Waring, 1807–1866, PUBL-0011-006-3, Alexander Turnbull Library

SHIPPING INTELLIGENCE.
ARRIVED.
March 12, schooner *Ariel*, 146, Mulholland, from Poverty Bay. Passengers—Mr. F. V. Martin, Mr. Harris, Messrs. P. Simpson, Arthur, and Albert, and 12 in the steerage.
March 15, brigantine *Sisters*, Clark, from Nelson Haven.
SAILED.
March 13, barque *Bolton*, 541, for Nelson Haven, with emigrants.

Newspaper announcement of the departure of the *Bolton* from Wellington, sailing to Nelson.

Papers Past, National Library of New Zealand, *New Zealand Gazette and Wellington Spectator*, Volume II, Issue 124, 16 March 1842

came on to snow on Sunday night and when we got up in the morning they had to scrape all the snow away from the doors and all the place was white, we had never seen it since we left England.

We all thought the minister could not come up but he came on a mule as there were no horses. We did not want a large party but the neighbours would have it, they all gave something, made or cooked or brought nearly all that was wanted. I had a pair of ducks, father gave me a suckling pig and I had some brandy sent me to make a sauce for the plum puddings. There were about 60 sat down to the wedding breakfast. Mr Ironside, the minister, said he had not seen so much snow since he left old England. He shook hands with me and said God meant us to be angels as there were four of us in white. My dear friend Mrs Ricketts, [later] my daughter's husband's mother, said as I had no mother or sister she would come and see that everything was properly done, and she did all she could to make us happy.

MARTHA ADAMS
LIFE AT REDWOOD

Martha Langley, known as Patty, married William Adams, a lawyer, in 1840, and ten years later they and their two children arrived in Nelson via New Plymouth, on the *Eden*, after six months at sea.

In 1852 William purchased a sheep run high in the upper Wairau, inland from Blenheim, which he named Redwood. Unfortunately the only living facilities for the pregnant Martha and her family was a 'mud hovel', in which they lived for five years. Two more sons, William and Percy, were born there. In 1857 William purchasd another run, on the northern banks of the Wairau, and named it Langley Dale after Martha's family.

In February 1852 William, having purchased a run and sheep far up in Marlborough, we were bodily moved by barge to the spot where no man's foot had ever been, and only Mr Wetherby and his one Maori shepherd. We took two men and furniture of limited and very plain description, and landing at once put the children and the goods under cover in a waggon, William and his men walking, a kind neighbour had lent me a horse. First night we camped at a hut of rushes with a rude chimney where we ate such dry food we had and with the children and dogs lay down to sleep on the mud floor in our blankets.

Next day we were all getting very weary when rain came on and

William said, 'Ride on Patty, you can't miss this narrow beaten track, till you come to a stream in a valley, then upwards and you will soon see some sort of shelter which is "our home".' I was always a fearless rider so off I went, and by and by through this wilderness of untrodden native grass, I took my horse through a respectable stream and then up and a mud hovel was before me. ...

Walls and chimney, spaces for a door and two windows, but no glass. Here dismounting I unsaddled my horse and tethered him and then ventured inside the walls, remembering the rain had increased. Here I found some wood on a rude fireplace, dirt everywhere and a pile of filthy sheep skins in one corner. Nothing else, the rain came through the two window spaces of two rooms and the open space for the door. I lighted a good fire and tucked up my habit and discovered a primitive broom of grass tied on to a stick with which I cleared a space near the fire for my two darlings to sit on when they arrived. Searching round I discovered a kettle and an old bucket with which I ran down the slope to the little brook 20 yards [18 m] in front, and soon had my kettle boiling just in time to receive the waggon, etc. This was indeed a change, but I lifted up my heart that God would always give me strength and spirits for all that might come in this strange rough new life.

And now looking back after years I think I may say in the darkest days I never quite lost heart.

When we had unpacked and the men had rigged a shelter for themselves William turned with his useful hands and nailed up rugs, etc. at windows and door and we were shut in.

For some time this primitive life continued. William and men and dogs killed two pigs, but one in our ignorance was not fit for food, the other was cut up on our one table in our one room and I fried it for food. Then I had to make soda cakes and bake them in our own oven, and so and so, till a happy day saw some men coming up the valley with the doors and windows, and we kept them till a second hut was made for the men, but which was not dry enough for them to go in for a long time. ...

Two, three, four, five years from entering Redwood and now my Cousin, Reverend Percy Langley, rector of Olney, sent us a worthy couple, woman cook, man farm servant, and times were smoother and one had a chance of sitting down to rest on week days and not only on Sundays as heretofore, after our weekly prayers, when dear Acton read us a chapter. Also sheep and wool bales having increased and a fat bullock sent to Nelson fetched £28. William felt he might buy a more civilised place so he and I went on horseback to look at land he afterwards named Langley after me, and we commenced to move downhill towards the great river Wairau, which bounded the new home. ...

So Willie and baby Percy and I walked by the side of the waggon to the end of the valley, and returned to feel how lonely it was. No horses, no cows, no sheep, no living things but our three selves for miles. When William gave me the parting kiss he said, 'You will be brave Patty as you always are, and you know there is nothing to hurt you, as there is nothing within miles of you. Good-bye.' And now I was really alone, for Willie was only little more than three and baby could but just toddle. There was nothing to cook, I had mutton left from yesterday, no milk, for cows were gone, few potatoes, and rice. It was weary work now with almost nothing to do but dress and feed the little ones and walk or sit on the high grassy banks of our picturesque river and sing to them. My Father had had a fine voice and a little of it dropped on me.

One day after another passed and we looked for the return of the waggon but no waggon came. Food got less and less. Anxious frightened days for me. No one came near us, we were too far away for me to walk and carry baby to our nearest neighbours eight or nine miles away. I measured out our bread and rice most carefully. And every Mother will know I ate little myself. We had heavy rain for days and this had raised the rivers and I guessed why no welcome waggon came with food. And one dark night, having put my hungry babes to bed I sat a while by the living-room fire safely thinking, when to my horror a knock came to the door. It was useless to open it, I had neither bed nor food to offer and as it was the back door I knew it was none of our well-to-do far off neighbouring sheep owners. I think my heart froze. Knock came again! Hastily I put out all fire and creeping on all fours crawled into the bedroom, for I was frightened lest the unknown might see my shadow. <u>What a night</u>! I felt it was very possible the tramps (for it could be none other else they would have spoken), [they] might break the tiny window, creep in and murder us all three. Do you think I could sleep. Round and round the mud cottage tramped the footsteps, now stopping, now continuing. No light inside or out, no Moon or stars, still damp rainy weather. If it was a traveller he could go to the men's cottage for shelter, but that was as bare of food as mine. Daylight at last. I kept the doors fast but could see no one about so bye and bye let the little starved darlings out to play in the welcome sunshine. As I had only a handful of rice left to cook in water I gave it to them and drank some water myself and prayed that it might sustain me, and I was so weak myself from want of food that I could understand the darlings crying, crying constantly as the day wore on and at last worn out, I'm afraid my tears mingled with theirs. ...

The sun was going down when oh, glad deliverance we saw the dray and party at bottom of the valley!!!! My sons for whom this is written, may none of you ever spend such a day as that. I could hardly kiss my beloved husband in my haste to tear down the bag with the bread and putting a piece in their tiny hands we went on with the party to our cottage, for we had hastened down the path to meet them. And the fire was lighted now there was mutton to cook, and tea made without milk, and oh, delicious bread and butter. What a feast as we sat around the blazing fire and talked and laughed in the sudden change of our feelings. Many, many

Martha Adams.
1/2-037842-F,
Alexander Turnbull Library

kisses for the darlings on father's knee and now they are asleep. We have no candles, but James the man, after his supper chopped a grand load of wood and a bright light we made. And now James is gone away to the men's cottage and my husband and I are alone, and I am sitting on his knee and his arm is around me before I tell him of my fright the night before. He kisses me and calls me 'Silly Patty' for it must have been all my fancy to think anyone could come like that. And he never knew me a coward before etc. More kisses — when suddenly, thrilling through our every nerve — came again — a knock at the back door. I slipped on to the floor in a heap and William grasping a thick stick from the hearth rushed to the door in the other back room and I nearly turned to stone lest he might be murdered. I sat by the ashes trembling. I heard angry words, etc. and feared more than once. Then the door was slammed and bolted and William returned and said it was a tramp that evidently had hidden in the tussocks all day and seeing no men about had meant to have frightened me into giving him food and lodging, but my husband catching him by the arm and holding the stick over him told him 'that he and James would both belabour him well in the morning if he found him about'. … So William came back to me and kissed up my tears and carried me off to bed, all the while taunting me in fun, for being a coward for the first time. And repeating, 'I would never have believed it, if anyone had told me.' But all the same he made up his mind not to leave me subject to another fit of cowardice. I think he hardly remembered how weak I was for want of necessary food, gradually reduced to simple water for one whole day.

ALICIA WILHEMINA CHITTY
'HIGH IDEALS AND FORTITUDE'

Alicia Wilhemina de Vere Hunt was born in County Tipperary, Ireland in 1858, the eldest daughter of Matthew de Vere Hunt of Huntsgrove, Templederry. Alicia, her parents, three brothers and sister arrived in Auckland in July 1872, on the Coronilla. *The family moved to Hamilton East, then to the main part of the growing town. In 1874, 15-year-old Alicia married Walter Chitty of Deal, England, who farmed 750 acres at Hukanui (today's Chartwell) and named it Brooklyn.*

In 1936, Alicia wrote an 'autobiographical sketch', a typescript of which is held in the Alexander Turnbull Library. In this she wrote, 'A record of pioneer women is often an account of repeated accomplishments of the seemingly impossible by people imbued by high ideals and fortitude.'

An enthusiastic farmer's wife needed to evolve methods of overcoming the lack of skilled tradesmen, scarcity of goods to which she had been accustomed, the rendering of first aid to man and animal, the dispensing of hospitality at any hour of day or night, being the tactful 'silent partner', yet the helpmate in the true sense of the word, and taking an interest in all developments and transactions connected with the home, farm and district. Some neighbouring women worked manually, with but scanty equipment. They carried baskets of eggs and walked many miles to the village in order to barter their goods for other necessities. They travelled by horseback.

Very little money changed hands in the stores. Trading was by barter. My father gave us a dray. This was the first in the district, and called for a celebration. It was the custom for settlers to combine and make life pleasanter for all. We had a picnic. The women clambered over the wheels, stood up in the dray, and were transported to a favourite spot. The earliest equipment in our home included a Colonial oven and big iron kettles, which could either be hung over the fire or rest on top of bars at the [the] top of [the] stove. Large iron boilers were used for the washing of clothes, and when required were erected outside the building on iron bars, which rested on big stones. In later years, when brick chimneys could be built, much improvement resulted, but still conditions remained more or less primitive.

The indoor bath was circular. It was about three or three and a half feet in diameter at the base and had sloping sides. These were about 1 foot in height. The shower had to be filled by bucket. It was suspended on a strong chain from a large hook in the ceiling. It was shaped like an oval tin hat box. It worked on the same principle as the cisterns in toilets of about 1910. But it was an indoor bath, with shower, even if it had to be filled by bucket. It was hung on the wall when not in use.

The lighting of the home was by candlelight and kerosene lamps. Candlesticks and lamps had to be cleaned daily. We purchased our candles, but a neighbour used to make her own. Dishes had to be washed in basins or small tubs. There were no indoor sinks. All the water was saved for watering plants. A well was dug and fitted with a windlass. The bucket was attached to the end of a long rope, wound, or unwound, onto a narrow barrel operated by a handle. I would not use the water for the washing of butter. We carried water for butter-making from a crystal clear spring about a quarter of a mile distant from the house.

Butter making was carried out in the dairy, where the fresh milk was first set in large shallow pans. There were no separators. Pans of milk were left undisturbed for stated periods and then the cream was skimmed off with a flat skimmer. Cream was collected for three days. The wooden churn containing wooden beaters, worked by a handle, was thoroughly sterilised with boiling water. It was later filled with cold water and chilled before the cream was poured in and beaten until the buttermilk was separated. The making of butter, during summer of the early pioneering days, was often done in the very early hours of the morning before the heat of the day. There were no refrigerators, and no ice for the pioneers.

Milking was done by hand. The bread was homemade, and meat was home grown, or farm-produced. When poultry was killed, the fine feathers were washed, dried and saved for stuffing pillows. When a sheep was slaughtered and made ready for the home, it was attached to a meat hook and rope. It was covered with a spotless white cloth something like a sheet, and hung in a high tree until it was required by the cook. The cook, whether mistress or maid, soon became proficient in the use of a meat saw or chopper.

The killing of a pig caused much extra work for women. Brawn was made, and bacon was cured. This was quite [a] task which lasted several weeks. First the meat was dry-salted. A little salt petre was added to the first dressing. Next, the meat had a mixture of dry salt and brown sugar rubbed into it. The process was repeated daily for a week. Following that, the meat was hung in a smokehouse similar to that which is used today for smoking fish in the Taupo area.

Branches of green ti-tree were used for smoking, an operation which lasted for weeks. The bacon finally hung on rafters in the kitchen and was not used for several months.

Maoris are, or were, particularly fond of bacon, and often a wahine would come to the kitchen door and glance longingly at the sides of bacon hanging from the rafters. Then with beguiling smiles she would say 'Mihi Chihee (the Maori pronounciation for Mrs Chitty), you any bacon …' then she would display such edibles as mushrooms, which were plentiful in the early days. In much later years, the Maoris would bring kits of luscious blackberries and expect something in exchange.

As the land was cultivated, it became productive of crops. We had a large acreage of oats and smaller fields of wheat and barley. Fruit trees were thriving, but we were impatient to have ample fruit for dessert. Walter followed the example of our neighbours and invested half-a-crown in the purchase of a bundle of blackberry plants. Throughout the remaining years, we spent thousands of pounds in trying to eradicate blackberry. If only we could have foreseen the effect of climate, it would have been different. ...

I learnt, like other women, to use hammer, nails, spade and such. I have also laid bricks.

Walter bred horses and sheep, in addition to the raising of crops. He was an early riser and energetic. This meant that extra helpers were employed. Farm hands had their main meals in the kitchen. During the harvesting and shearing season, a never-ending supply of refreshments was provided by the housewife, and sent to the fields or sheds where men were employed or voluntarily assisting. There was a co-operative spirit among neighbours. Pioneering days were exceptionally busy periods for all the women on farms.

When horses had to be taken to a Hamilton forge to be shod, I sometimes assisted by either riding, or driving and leading the horse which had to be shod. The forge was located in Hamilton East, near the Royal Hotel, It was conducted by George E. Pearson, son of a carpenter, G.S. Pearson, the man who had the honour of having built the first house in Hamilton. In later years, a blacksmith brought his gear to 'Brooklyn' and there shod our animals.

It was a very busy, happy life, though one sometimes longed for the comforts of the homeland. One took pride in developing farm and district and in helping those who were ill and helping the furthering of social activities. At times, though very tired, one seemed to be endowed with extra strength when there was an emergency.

My first child was born on my twenty first birthday. All told we were blessed with nine children, and when the second youngest of these had entered her teens, we were able to provide a home at 'Brooklyn' for four nephews and a niece who had been left motherless. The mother had died in childbirth and her children were orphaned.

Confinements always took place in the home. There was always a doctor in Hamilton, but never until very recent years were there sufficient physicians to meet the needs of the growing town. There was a midwife, a Mrs Lees, in the district, but again she might have been needed in two places in the same time. Roads were unformed or were mere tracks, and travel was slow.

Though I gained experience 'the hard way', it has been my privilege to assist many sick people and to render aid in time of accidents. The use of antiseptics, home made bandages and sling, castor oil, mustard plasters and fomentations applied with a little common sense, saved many a doctor's bill.

> Sir,—We, the undersigned passengers per ship Coronilla, are unwillingly that this opportunity should pass without the expression of our thanks for the many kindnesses we have received from you; also our satisfaction at the very able manner in which you have conducted the affairs of the ship. We have always found you as ready to assist in our amusements as you were to do anything possible for our comfort in the bad weather, and although the voyage has been a long one, still we have had no cause of complaint whatever. Wishing you many happy and prosperous voyages.—We are, sir, yours respectfully, Mathew De Vere Hunt for self wife and five children; J. H. Hemus and wife, Easton Salter, Margaret Ryan.

Alicia's father, Mathew De Vere Hunt, was one of the people who wrote to the captain of the *Coronilla* to thank him for his safe passage to New Zealand.

Papers Past, National Library of New Zealand, *Auckland Star*, Volume III, Issue 784, 22 July 1872

What's a fomentation?

A poultice, which is a soft, moist mass of material applied to the body to relieve soreness and inflammation.

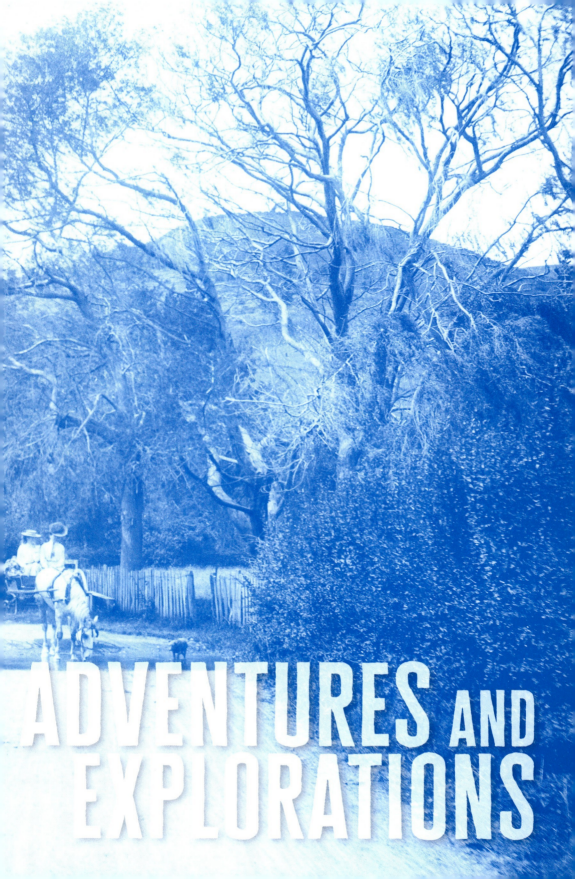

SARAH MATHEW

CLIMBING THE VOLCANO OF RANGITOTO

Sarah Mathew was born in London and married her cousin Felton in Sydney in 1835. The couple was present at the founding of Auckland in 1840, when Felton was Acting Surveyor-General of the infant colony. Sarah and Felton travelled together around Northland, and they lived in Auckland until 1845.

I think it was in the second year of the Settlement, that the city being now all laid out, the streets marked out and named, the sale of the Allotments took place, and my husband bought two of them, in order to include the pretty spot on which our tents had first stood, and then our house was begun. A ship came in from Van Diemen's land or Tasmania as it is now called with a cargo of superior timber for building purposes, & of this our house was built. ... But we continued to inhabit our little Warre [whare] for some time after our return from the cruise to the South, making several expeditions by land exploring the country round Auckland, sometimes on foot, but generally on horseback, or in our boat, on the Manukao [Manakau] or Waitemata. One of our most fatiguing expeditions was to the top of the highest of the Volcanic Peaks on the Island of Rangitoto: we were accompanied on this occasion by our young friend, John du Moulin, who was indeed at that time one of our family, Captain Rough, the Harbour Master, and Captain England, a retired officer who had come out to settle in the new Colony, poor fellow he was killed by the Natives a few years afterwards. But at that time, all was bright & hopeful, and no one had the least apprehension of hostilities. We started early in our boat, taking provisions with us, it was a beautiful day I remember in early spring time, when all the trees and shrubs were in flower, the bright yellow balls or tufts of the Acacias, with numbers of those beautiful birds the Tui, which specially affect these trees as if aware that their shining black plumage appeared to great advantage in contrast with the golden blossoms and graceful foliage of the Acacia, then the Rata with its small red flowers, & the Fuchsias with varied flowers, red or white or purple, & largest of all the Pohutukawa, which grows quite down to the coast covered with large crimson tufted blossoms shaped like a bottle-brush; but besides all these, & climbing over all, are the largest flowered white clematis I ever saw; and many other shrubs we noticed, as we clambered over the broken masses of Scoria of which the whole island seems to be composed, track or path there was none, after we left the Beach; and the extraordinary richness of the vegetation covering all this bed of Scoria was remarkable. We were more than 3 hours in the ascent, every step over huge masses of brittle substance, sometimes so thin as to break under our feet, every interstice filled with fern or shrubs and parasitic plants, which were in some places a help, their tough streamers giving us something to hold on by, when the Scoria & broken rocks rolled from our feet. The height is by measurement only 900 or a

Sarah Louise Mathew, photographed in the 1860s. Sarah would have been in her 50s.

Sir George Grey Special Collections, Auckland Libraries, 7-A11646 thousand feet [300 m] above sea level, but the nature of the ground to be trodden, & the steepness of the ascent, makes it more fatiguing than many higher mountains; and there were deep hollows, extinct craters, which we had to go round, or descend into & ascend on the other side, here the ground was bare of all vegetation, & was only a mass of fine cinders, into which the feet would sink, as on a shingly beach, so we tried to keep to the steeper parts of the hill. The heat was excessive & not a drop of water was to be found all through that toilsome day. At last we reached the summit, all quite exhausted, & sat down to rest and breathe. We found the top of the mountain was a deep hollow and surrounded by irregular Peaks, apparently formed by the action of the Volcano, throwing up heaps of ashes or scoria in several directions, probably at different periods; it must have been long extinct by the quantity and size of the vegetation; but what a wonderfully extensive view we gained from this point, all the Firth of Thames studded with its islands, the great and little Barrier islands with their rich Copper mines, the dense forest of the island Waiheke, the Mercury isles [sic], Coromandel with its gold diggings, then suspected but all as yet unknown, & then Kareho sleeping in the sunshine & the little busy hive we had left this morning scarcely to be distinguished from the unknown forest. The wind blew so strongly on the summit, we could scarcely stand, & after resting awhile, and making a fire of the dead wood, which burned for some days, we began our descent, trying what appeared an easier way, than that by which we ascended; it seemed from the top of the mountain as if a stream of Scoria and stones had poured over the lip of the crater, quite down to the shore: but this was broken by deep fissures, and in places so covered with vegetation that our progress was often impeded, the sharp rocks & scoria had worn my boots to pieces, & my dress of grey merino was torn in shreds, struggling through the thorny brush wood, & by the sharp edges of the rocks — thankful

> **What's an interstice?**
>
> A very small space. Sarah would have been talking about the small cracks, crevices and holes that she would have had to navigate on her walks.

was I to see the shore & boat at last, where we had some wine, but no water had been found, tho' the men left with the boat had searched half round the island for some spring or stream: this absence of water would account for there being no living creature on it; we saw nothing, not even a bird. We were all quite exhausted, & after a short rest returned to Auckland. It was quite dark when we landed, and we had scarcely reached our house, when my husband was taken with faintness & shivering which alarmed me very much. I sent for Dr Johnson who administered brandy, & sat with him some time after he got to bed; he told me it was exhaustion from over-exertion, & that he would be well in the morning, which was indeed the case after a night's rest. This alarm quite cured my fatigue, I watched the greater part of the night, and felt no want of sleep, tho' previously in the boat I had scarcely been able to keep my eyes open.

This image is from an original sketch by Sarah of her home in Auckland, with St Paul's Church at the rear.

Sir George Grey Special Collections, Auckland Libraries, 7-A4046

CAROLINE CHEVALIER

AN INHOSPITABLE INN

Caroline (née Wilkie) was married to the artist Nicholas Chevalier, and often accompanied him on his journeys around Australia and New Zealand, which they visited in the 1860s. One expedition with her artist husband and a companion called Scott involved a journey from Canterbury to Westland across the Harper Pass, in 1866. After struggling down the wild river flats of the Taramakau River into Westland, the party approached a junction with the new coach road over Arthur's Pass. The prospect of civilisation, however, was quickly dispelled as they found themselves in an inn which catered for gold-miners on the journey through the Southern Alps.

We journeyed till sunset & arrived at a small accommodation house, where the road forks to the Otira Gorge. We had struck the coach road which had been made by Arthur Dobson, & whose name was given to the pass over the Otira Gorge. Having been directed that this house existed, we were all looking forward for a most delightful supper & bed. Coming up to it, it really looked most inviting, a pretty little place with a square foot & a skillion back. Of course of wood but a big chimney. The proprietor, a young fellow,

> **What's a skillion?**
>
> A skillion is a lean-to attached to a building to provide extra room, in Caroline's time especially as a kitchen.

This image was painted by Nicholas Chevalier in London, ten years after he and Caroline had made the journey from Christchurch to the Hokitika in 1866. It depicts them crossing the Taramakau River with their guide, Mr Scott.

'Crossing the Taramakau River', 1876, London, by Nicholas Chevalier. Gift of Mrs Caroline Chevalier, the artist's widow, England, 1919. 1919-0002-14, Museum of New Zealand Te Papa Tongarewa

came out immediately to welcome us, but what was my disappointment to find the only bed room he had, was just taken by a man & his wife & three children, a rather large party for a little place of a few feet square, & a kind of wooden stretcher or two, no other furniture. Still it was a covering from rain. They were common people journeying on the road to Hokitika, there hoping to find work or make a fortune digging.

We were all too tired to travel farther & the horses done up, so Nicolas decided to take what we could get, & really it was much worse than camping. The house consisted of a front room for eating & a bar, over it the one sleeping room, behind, a skillion kitchen with a big fire, & one end of this skillion had a kind of shed, or one would call it a stable. It was divided from the kitchen by boards or slabs about an inch from each other, & against this was put two flat slabs to form shelves for people to sleep on. The proprietor showed us these with great satisfaction & considered they were most desirable sleeping accommodation & I have no doubt asked a good price. I know he asked a very big price for some oats for our horses, & gave them very little. We had to accept this or go on & find a camping ground & it was late & we were done up. So we unpacked & stored the things in the shed & the horses were hobbled, but from that moment N. had no rest, for horses & saddles were most valuable in these quarters, & there were a set of horrible fellows, squatting about drinking & smoking, & they would think nothing of taking horses or any thing they could lay their hands on. Indeed during the next few months occurrences showed that desperate characters were on those very roads, for poor Arthur Dobson mentioned above was murdered by a set of ruffians who mistook him for a store keeper returning with gold dust. And one of the dreadful rascals turned Queen's evidence & acknowledged they had killed 20 or 30 (I think) poor unfortunate people. You can imagine that the faces of these kind of men gave you fear, but I had no idea that they might go off with the horses. Had they done so, we were undone. We got a kind of supper, & some tea, & Scott had his pipe with the party of diggers & rascals in the kitchen. Our supper was taken with the family party, & I really was greatly interested with the poor woman & her nice little children. What a life the poor creature [had] & what became of her I have often wondered. The terrible things I heard of after, frightened me for any women's lives thrown into such places.

Naturally we hoped to be down — I can't say go to bed — early & we took our blanket, & the man gave us each a dirty thing which we could not use. We entered our apartment — earth floor, old rubbish about, wood & some tools. I managed to scramble with assistance to the upper berth or rather shelf, & lay me down & N. took the under one. But sleep — how could one, there between the inch chinks I looked at these men, many half drunk, all noisy, some miserable, some wild, there were about a dozen. They were drinking beer I suppose and smoking. The big fire blazed & made the darkness cheerful, for there was but one candle. Their

Caroline Chevalier in her mid to late-20s.

Batchelder & O'Neill, fl 1857–1875, Haast family: photographs. PA2-0247, Alexander Turnbull Library

conversation was not agreeable, some were most quarrelsome, & we unfortunate people seemed the theme of a deal of unpleasantness. We were talked of indirectly as confounded aristocrats, and upstarts & every name they could think of because I had not gone in and sat down with them, & I began to wonder how the night would end, when suddenly about 10 o'clock the proprietor opened the door, & shouted 'now then all out'. Then began a scrimmage some would go & some would not, but he absolutely drove them, little fellow as he was, & then he went out himself & turned the key & we heard him mount a horse & ride away. Now we thought we should have a quiet night,

Scott was to sleep in some out house & after N. had gone out & seen all four horses he was more content & we composed ourselves for a sleep. Alas, alas — in less than ten minutes the place was alive, not with people but with rats — rats that rushed up & down on the table over the chairs along the rafters all around the fire & packed along close to the chinks, squeaking and rushing. This was too dreadful. I could see them of course plainly, I knocked, I called out, but they cared for nothing, and nothing could be done but get a candle & sit up till morning, and this we did until the proprietor returned & his presence seemed to drive the beasts away. It was one of the most dreadful nights I have passed. Camping out was peaceful & healthful compared to it. I never shall forget those horrid creatures sitting on the table on their hind legs & eating every scrap & crumb they could find & fighting with each other. New Zealand is a terrible place for rats, they say they go about in shoals under the ground & have their exits here and there. It is so extraordinary, because New Zealand is like Ireland & has no reptiles, & yet the rat swarms.

We were thankful when day light returned, & as soon as we had had some hot coffee, and some nasty bread and butter for which we paid exorbitantly we bade adieu to the accommodation house to which we had so looked forward as a quiet resting place.

ELEANOR ADAMS
CHILD EXPLORER ON THE MILFORD TRACK

Eleanor Adams was just 11 years old when she walked what is now the world-famous Milford Track in Fiordland, in 1888. Eleanor joined a survey party including her father, Charles Adams, then chief surveyor of the Otago province, and Quinton Mackinnon, who gave his name to the main pass of the track. Their journey from Milford Sound to Lake Te Anau, which today takes guided walkers travelling east to west just four days, took around four weeks.

It was only a short while after my Father had returned from the Sounds where he had surveyed the Sutherland Falls — finding them to be only 1904 ft. [580 m] high instead of about 4000 [1220 m] much to the disappointment of the discoverers — that he and I left the Bluff in one of the Union Co.'s boats to return to Milford early in 1889.

We had a very rough trip, and my Father being a very bad sailor was very glad to get into the perfectly calm waters of the Sound in the late afternoon. There were a number of English tourists on board and they were delighted that the ship had to call at Milford to land my Father and myself there giving them a chance to see Milford Sound, but the Captain was not at all pleased as it delayed his arrival in Melbourne. We had expected to find two survey parties awaiting us at Milford but there was no sign of them.

Taken in 1911, this image shows the Ball huts in which Eleanor and her father would have stayed on their journey.

'Ball huts', Fred Brockett, photographer, A.003230, Museum of New Zealand Te Papa Tongarewa

However, the Captain put us ashore in one of the ship's boats as soon as we reached the head of the Sound, and as soon as possible put to sea again. The tourists were distressed at leaving us there by ourselves — my father looked frail after the rough sea trip and I was only eleven — and they persuaded the Captain to let us have some food to take ashore with us. Sutherland was away and I never met him at all — but he had left his hut open for us to use.

My father and I watched the steamer until out of sight. It was terribly lonely with not another soul there and surrounded by such huge mountains and thick bush to the water's edge. Luckily I did not know how anxious my Father was at the non-arrival of the survey parties. They had planned to be at Milford days before we arrived — but bad weather and numerous avalanches near the Pass had delayed them.

We went to bed early — at least I did — and in the early hours of the morning my Father heard a coo-ee from across the water and knew that at least some of the party had arrived safely. Soon after daylight a tiny little canvas boat came over, and I think we started off the same day.

That little canvas boat was the only boat we had and it held only 2 or 3 at a time and it took some time getting the party over the river or lakes. Someone had to squat down in the bow and watch for any snags — Lake Ada was full of them — that might hole the canvas. We had a very rough walk from the Sound to the Ball (now called Quentin) huts and it took a long time getting us up Lake Ada in the canvas boat — I think some of the party scrambled round the lake. It was lucky there were the two huts near the Sutherland Falls for we had to stay many days there on account of bad weather. The huts were very primitive affairs but they, as well as Sutherland's hut, all had some very pretty curtains and I wondered where the material came from. One of the surveyors told me that it had been torn from a French Countess's dress, when she had tried to walk up from Milford to see the Falls, she had returned to the Tourist ship with only the lining of her dress left and no shoes.

One day while we were at the Ball huts we had a frightening thunder storm — in the flashes of lightning the mountains seemed to tower over us.

At the Ball huts the bush rats were dreadful but luckily I was not afraid of mice and rats, but all the same did not like their running all over me as soon as the lights were out. I begged a yard of the white calico — used for the survey pegs — from my father and cut a good many holes in it so that I could breathe, and put it right over my head. I felt quite happy that way. During this bad weather my Father was quite anxious and wondered when we could get over the Pass.

One day we saw the Sutherland Falls — we were about quarter

of a mile away I think, but we were covered with spray. I lost all sense of distance among those huge mountains and thought I could throw a stone into the pool at the foot of the Falls.

At last a good day came and the party for Te Anau and ourselves started off over the Pass. It was hard work pulling ourselves up through the heavy bush but above the bush line the way looked very dangerous, especially skirting Mt Balloon where the rocky ground was all slimy with moss and water. Quintin Mackinnon roped me to himself and my Father and we all got safely to the top of the Pass. The little tarn on top was called after me — Lake Ella.

Looking down the thousands of feet into the valley we had left was awe-inspiring. The only way I could look was to lie down flat and pull myself to the edge of the cliff and get my Father to hold my ankles!

> **What's a tarn?**
>
> A tarn is a small mountain lake.

We camped somewhere near the foot of the Pass and all night long were kept awake with avalanches falling. Just over the Pass above the heavy bush we went through acres of the large flowered houhere or ribbonwood — it was like a cherry orchard in Spring.

Going down the Clinton Valley was the easiest part of the journey and very lovely. When we came to the Clinton River it was a raging torrent with huge boulders, and the younger of the Quill brothers carried me across. We could see the river coming out from a huge ice cave at the head of the valley, and also saw an avalanche falling near.

The track to Te Anau was fairly level and we caught lovely glimpses of the Clinton River with its clear greenish waters. The native birds were so tame, and the little robins would come a perch on our toes and hats while we had our meals, ready for any crumbs. And nearly always while my Father was surveying a robin would perch on his hat or theodolite. Wood hens were plentiful in the Clinton Valley and would run off with anything bright they could find in your tent. If you imitated their call they would come right up to you.

Above the bush line at the Pass there were many native flowers — unfortunately I did not know the names of many of them. I saw one big white mountain daisy and mountain lily and at the Sound the rata was ablaze.

The bush was magnificent — huge trees with their trunks covered with lovely mosses and ferns and long trails of moss hanging from their boughs. Wherever you put a foot down you had to tread on lovely kidney and other ferns and mosses and masses of tiny native plants. And waterfalls and lovely mountain streams were everywhere. I think it took us three weeks to reach Lake Te Anau, then we had three days in Mackinnon's boat on a perfectly calm lake rowing all the way and camping two nights on lovely little beaches — once on the West side and once on the East.

Mackinnon shot some duck and cooked our dinners over a fire in a kerosene tin in the boat. One day we stopped under a huge bluff for our dinner and when we dropped our duck bones over the side of the boat we could see them sinking down and down for ages — the water was so wonderfully clear.

We stayed at a sheep station on the East side of the Lake for the night and next day we rode on horse back to Lumsden station where we got a train to Dunedin.

'Sutherland Fall, 1904 feet, near Milford Sound'. This image was taken in 1888.

Burton Brothers Studio, 1888, purchased 1981 with New Zealand Lottery Board fund, MA_I246155, Museum of New Zealand, Te Papa Tongarewa

Lake Ella, Mt Balloon and Jervois Glacier from top of McKinnon Pass, Milford Track. Eleanor's father named Lake Ella after her.

'Milford Sound' by Muir & Moodie Studio, purchased 1998 with New Zealand Lottery Grands Board fund. PS.001281, Museum of New Zealand Te Papa Tongarewa

WAR AND DISASTER

ELIZABETH HOLMAN
THE EVACUATION OF WHANGAREI

During her 93 eventful years, Elizabeth Holman experienced a wide and varied slice of colonial life in New Zealand and Australia. Raised in Sydney where her father was Official Assignee, Elizabeth first crossed the Tasman on an expedition to extract kauri spars from the Hokianga in 1840. She returned to New Zealand the next year and married Henry Holman in Kororareka (now Russell, Bay of Islands). During their 53 years of marriage the couple lived in Auckland, Sydney, the Thames goldfields and around Northland. Among the major events in her reminiscences, held in the Alexander Turnbull Library, is the sacking of Kororareka by Hone Heke and his followers in 1845, and the subsequent evacuation of Whangarei when settlers there feared attack by Maori. Written by Elizabeth in a 'stream of consciousness' style, this extract has been punctuated to make the story easier to follow.

Elizabeth's reminiscences were adapted into a biography by Florence Keene and published in 1972 under the title With Flags Flying.

> **Sacking a town**
>
> When a town was 'being sacked' it meant it was being robbed of goods and valuables.

At that time there were a lot of mischievous people about who took delight in making the Natives discontented putting foolish ideas into their heads. Those American Whaler Sailors did a deal of mischief that way particularly in Auckland. The Maoris began to

Elizabeth Holman.
96/13, PH-2001-4-2,
Auckland War Memorial Museum
Tamaki Paenga Hira

think they were far better off in the old Bay of Islands Whaling time and it was these together with the French Whaler sailors, a bad lot, [who] would tell the Maoris that it was through that flag flying up there that they could not now do as they formerly used to do. These worthless men so influenced a lot of the Natives that it became a serious matter and at last they did cut down the flag & early one morning the Natives made an attack on the farther end of the town close to the Church. Captn. Robertson of the *Hazard* landed with his sailors to support the soldiers & 13 of the poor sailors were slain and Captn Robertson had a bullet in his arm. While this was going on Hone

Heke and his men cut the flag staff down. The Europeans collected in a fortified house on the beach and defended themselves for some time. After three hours fighting the Natives asked for time to be allowed to carry off their wounded. Taking advantage of this truce the Europeans thought it best to escape while they could and there were three ships in the bay into which all the people of Kororareka crowded and gave the place up to Maoris. As soon as all were on board the Maoris came from the hills and burnt & plundered the town.

I could tell a lot about this. Mrs. Ford & the Dr. with their 4 children and servant were hurrying through the town when it was being sacked by the Natives and things lying about in the streets. One of the little girls picked up a jug. Of course it was taken from her. The child cried and Hone Heke came to the child putting the jug in her hand saying she shall have it (and they took that jug to Auckland and it was always called the Hone Heke jug). When they reached the ship in the harbour they saw their house in flames as well as the rest of the town and hundreds of people had nothing but what they stood up in and arrived in Auckland in that plight in March 1845.

Well I must now tell you how we poor folks in Whangarei fared. Nearly all the Maoris about there were friendly but there were some down the river, [in] a large settlement in Matarau that were not. Our friendly natives said we had better leave and go to Auckland, that if the Natives took Kororareka they would not answer for our safety. So my husband said he would go to Auckland and get the Governor to let him have some sort of a vessel and bring it to Whangarei to take us all away. He left at once in some small boat but before he left there were 4 or 5 Chiefs who promised to keep watch over us all and in case of any immediate danger were to let us know. I was to stay with the Mair family until my husband's return with the vessel to take us all away. He had only left a few days when the Native Chiefs came to Mr. Mair and told him that we and all the settlers must get away at once. There were about 50 in all at that time scattered about the settlement and strange to say that day a small craft called the *Trial* with two men on board of her (she was about 12 tons in size) came up the river as far as Graham's town. How it was I can't remember but I think some natives went on board and they were frightened and left the vessel in their boat and the day after that we were all at tea when we heard a frightful yelling. The door was thrown open and the room filled with natives. They all had guns & spears and the old Chief Tanru rushed about saying Te Horoma Whiena and caught hold of me & threw his blanket round me baby and all for I held tight to my baby. He ran away with me down to the river and put me into his canoe. It was quite dark — you may imagine my feelings better than I can describe them. The old Cannibal had promised my husband that he would take care of me and all the time I was under his blanket he kept jabbering to me words of comfort it seemed but it might have been quite the reverse for all I knew as I did not then understand one word of their language or very little. He and his men took me & some others down the river and put us on board this Craft that the men had left and during the night all the settlers came on board.

    Towards morning Mr. Mair came with William Poe, the chief who would not leave Mr. Mair until he saw him safely on board. They came down the river in a boat of Mr. Mair's and when all the settlers were on board, 47 or 50, the Native Chiefs said get away as quickly as possible which we did. We were just packed like sardines in a box. We were three days getting to Kawau Island and it came on to blow. We must all have gone to the bottom of the sea during this time. We had no food and we reached the Kawau in a most pitiable state.

    Mr. Leather was living there at that time managing a copper mine. He received us in a most kindly way and did everything to comfort the weak & suffering, turned out of his cottage of two rooms for the females and set his men to work to prepare food for the starving lot. It was here that my husband picked us up in the *British Queen*, a craft of about 30 tons. He had heard that we had been driven away but how he heard I can't remember. My husband thought most likely we might have reached the Kawau and so went in or round that way

Whangarei in the 1880s.

KEENE_037_036, Florence Keene Collection, Heritage Collection, Whangarei Libraries

and thankful enough I was to see him. I was in a very weak state and had it not been for Mrs. John Gorrie I should have died on the way. My poor child was between 8 & 9 months old. None of the people had anything in the shape of clothing but what we had on our back. ...

All the Wives and families ... were to stay in Auckland. Auckland at that time was in a great state of commotion. Nothing in the shape of business was done. I really do not know how all the people lived. The English Church St Pauls was blockaded & several block houses were erected and guards of soldiers to watch all day and all night around them. Many times false alarms have filled the church with women & children in the middle of the night. After the taking of the Pa, Ruapekapeka, Heke became anxious for peace. All his people were tired of fighting and beginning to feel the want of food. Heke & Kawiti, a Chief that had always helped him wrote to the Governor asking forgiveness and promising to behave well in the future. Pardon was granted and peace was made in January 1846.

RHODA COOTE
THE 1855 EARTHQUAKE IN WELLINGTON

Married to a British Army officer, Rhoda Carleton Coote came out to New Zealand in 1852 and lived in Wellington for seven years, before returning to England. When her husband Henry retired, they returned to New Zealand and lived on farms in Canterbury and the Wairarapa until Henry's death in 1867.

Rhoda was living in Wellington when a big earthquake struck just after nine o'clock on the evening of 23 January 1855. The main quake and its aftershocks changed the face of the Wellington waterfront, lifting up large areas of swamp around Clyde Quay and raising the shoreline of the harbour by up to three metres. The sole fatality of the quake was Baron Charles von Alzdorf, who was an important businessman in the growing town. His twostorey hotel on the Wellington waterfront collapsed and killed him during the shake of 1855.

In January 1855 we experienced a severe earthquake, which was a great shock to our appreciation of New Zealand and truly alarming. On January 23rd after a very windy and boisterous day, about 9 o'clock in the evening we were startled by a rumbling noise, followed instantly by a tremendous shaking of everything about us. Floor upheaving, tables and chairs rocking and everything breakable crashing. The first shock lasted several minutes they say, and threw down every chimney in Wellington as well as many buildings and did a great deal of damage in the town. We were in a low wooden house close under the hill, so it only threw down our chimney and broke our lamps and most of our glass, but so severe were the shocks that we left the house and stayed outside a great part of the night, though it was raining slightly. The animals were greatly frightened, horses galloped about and the fowls began cackling, and our poor servant Eliza came in to us and we all stayed out for several hours. A party of soldiers came over from the barracks to see if we wanted help and Colonel MacCleverty kindly came to ask after us. The shocks continued more or less violent, but none like the first, till between 3 and 4 o' clock, and then became less frequent, and morning broke to gladden our hearts but to reveal a miserable picture. The first thing we noticed was the extreme lowness of the tide; the sand extended far beyond its usual limits, and then all at once it was covered again by the sea, this advancing and receding of the tide took place three times in twenty minutes, and eventually left the harbour raised about three feet. The Beach where all the shops are situated was a miserable picture, few houses uninjured whilst many were perfect wrecks, and the contents of many of the shops were floating about on the water or thrown up on the shore. But only one life was lost and that was Baron Dalzdorf [von Alzdorf] of the hotel, and he was in a very delicate state and the shock may have affected his heart, not but which the wall of the room he was in fell. The Cliffords' house was left with only one room safe, and they went to the MacClevertys' — the Featherstons' was also very shaky and Mrs. Featherston and the baby came to us, but the Dr. would not move. Government House and the Bank, only just finished were much damaged, and all through the town scarcely any escaped. From the country strange stories came of the ground opening and engulfing cows etc., but I believe imagination was very active in originating most of the mischief reported, but it was quite terrible enough, and for days the earth continued to vibrate every now and then and we did not dare undress and go to bed for three nights. Then by degrees the shocks became very light and less frequent and we resumed our usual mode of life.

Sunday 28th. The effect of the earthquake was still so great on the nerves of the good people of Wellington that the Service this morning was held outside the Church, the Clergyman thinking it right to be prepared for what might happen, which I thought a very bad example to set to his Congregation, but we had a very good sermon, it seems, with a short service. It was the same in the afternoon, the people were all outside the church — happily it was fine. I have not mentioned that finding houses so scarce and extravagant in price, Henry sent home for one soon after we arrived, and just about this time we heard of the arrival of the ship the *Royal Stuart,* in which it was, first

A depiction of a landslip caused by the 1855 Wellington earthquake.

Gold, Charles Emilius, 1809–1871.
B-103-016, Alexander Turnbull Library

Newspaper report about the 1855 earthquake.

ENZC18550127.2.7, Papers Past, *Nelson Examiner and New Zealand Chronicle*, Vol. Xiii, Issue 705, 27 January 1855

EARTHQUAKE AT WELLINGTON.

We have received the painful intelligence that the city of Wellington and its neighbourhood has again been visited with a most severe earthquake; and we find that the shocks which have been experienced in Nelson during the present week, like the shocks of October, 1848, have been but the half spent wave which first rose somewhere on the shores of the southern extremity of Cook's Straits, but the exact locality of which we have yet to learn. To the arrival last night of H.M. Sloop Pandora, we owe the receipt of this intelligence; and Captain Drury, with a kindness we can scarcely sufficiently acknowledge, has placed at our disposal a copy of his journal, which narrates the whole calamity as it passed under his eye.

at Canterbury and now on January 29th it reached Wellington and was pronounced to be of all kinds the most suited to stand the shock of earthquakes, wooden walls with iron posts. Strange indeed that it should have come at such an opportune time. It was some time before we could get either plan or model of it so that days elapsed without anything being done, and now alas a very disagreeable quarrel arose between the Provincial Government and Military Authorities about some tents required for the people rendered houseless by the earthquake, which led to a most uncalled for attack of the former on Colonel MacCleverty. This became so warm that the cause of it all was forgotten, making this time most trying in every way to the society of the place, which never quite recovered the moral shock though the physical one soon passed off.

LADY MARY ANNE BARKER
THE GREAT SNOW OF 1867

Lady Mary Anne Barker (later Lady Broome) is one of the best-known chroniclers of life in colonial New Zealand. Her books, including Station Life in New Zealand, *deal mainly with her experiences on a large sheep station in the Canterbury high country. She came to New Zealand after marrying Frederick Napier Broome in 1865, following the death of her first husband, Sir George Barker. They lived on the Steventon station in the Malvern Hills, inland from Christchurch, which they renamed Broomielaw.*

The heavy snow of the winter of 1867 was disastrous for many Canterbury runs. While five days of steady snow weakened the vast flocks, it was the warm wind and heavy rain of the ensuing thaw that caused most of the stock fatalities, as paddocks flooded and sheep drowned. The lambing season had just begun, and Lady Barker reports that 3000 lambs died on the station as a result of the storm.

It was no surprise to me to see snow falling steadily next morning, but it was disagreeable to find there was very little mutton in the house, and that it was quite likely the shepherd would wait for the weather to clear before starting across the hills and swamps between us and the little homestead where the woolshed stood, and from whence the business of the station was carried on.

The three gentlemen lounged about all day and smoked a good

deal. They told me afterwards how bitterly they regretted not having made some preparation in the way of at least bringing in fuel, or putting extra food out for the fowls, etc. But each said to the other every five minutes, 'Oh, you know snow in New Zealand never lasts,' though their experience was only a very few years old. It was short commons that second day, and I thought sadly that the dray would have only reached Christchurch that evening! We all felt depressed, and, as no one had any use for depression up that valley, the sensation was quite new to us.

> **Short commons**
>
> When Lady Barker talks about 'short commons', she is referring to the shortage of food. A ratafia biscuit was an almond-flavoured biscuit.

It was not until we met on the third morning, however, that we at all acknowledged our fears. By this time, the snow was at least four feet deep in the shallowest places, and still continued to fall steadily. It was impossible to see even where the fowl-house and pig-sties stood, on the weather side of the house. All the great logs of wood lying about waiting to be cut up were hidden, so was the little shed full of coal. A smooth high slope, like a hillock, stretched out from the outer kitchen door, which could not be opened that morning, out into the floating whiteness. All our windows were nearly blocked up and became quite so by the evening, and no door except one, which opened inwards, could be used. And there was literally no food in the house. The tea we had at breakfast was merely coloured hot water, and we each had a couple of picnic biscuits. For dinner there was a little rice and salt. Imagine six people to be fed every day, and an empty larder and store-room!

The day after that my maids declined to get up, declaring they preferred to 'die warm'; so I took them in a sardine each, a few ratafia biscuits, and a spoonful of apricot jam. These were our own rations for that day. We had by that time broken up every box for fuel, and only lighted a fire in the kitchen, where also a solitary candle burned. ...

By Friday morning the maids, still in bed, were asking tearfully, 'And oh! when do you think we'll be found, mum?' Whereas my anxiety was to find something to feed them with! We shook out a heap of discarded flour-bags and got, to our joy, quite a plateful of flour, and a careful smoothing out of the lead lining of old tea-chests yielded a few leaves, so we had gridlecakes and tea that day. I was very unhappy about the dogs: the horses were out on the run as usual, so it was no use thinking of them.

On Saturday there was literally nothing at all in the house (which was quite dark, remember), and my three starving men roped themselves together and struggled out, tunnelling through the snow, in the direction where they thought the fowl-house must lie. After a couple of hours' hard work they hit upon its roof, tore off some of the wooden shingles, and captured a few bundles of feathers, which were what my poor dear hens were reduced to. However, there was a joyful struggle back, and after some hasty preparation the fowls were put into a saucepan with a lump of snow, for there was no water to be got anywhere, and a sort of stew resulted, of which we thankfully partook. This heartened up the gentlemen to make another sally to the stockyard in search of the cows. The clever creatures had kept moving round and round as the snow fell, so as to make a sort of wider tomb for themselves, and they were alive, though mere bundles of skin and bone. They were dragged by ropes to the stable and there fed with oaten hay. It was no question of milking the poor things, for they were quite dry.

Next day the dogs were dug out, but only one young and strong one survived. Two more were alive, but died soon after.

On Sunday it had ceased snowing and the

Mary Anne Barker and her husband Frederick Napier Broome. Mary Anne was most likely around 35 years of age when this photograph was taken.

1/2-043105-F, Alexander Turnbull Library

wind showed signs of changing. I struggled a yard or two out of the house, as it was such a blessing to get into daylight again. My view was of course much circumscribed, as I could only see up and down the 'flat', as the valley was called. But it all looked quite different; not a fence or familiar landmark to be seen on any side. If I could have been wafted to the top of the mountain from which we saw the sun rise the summer before, what a white world should I have beheld! And if I could have soared still higher and looked over the whole of the vast Canterbury Plains, I should have been gazing at the smooth winding-sheet of half a million of sheep, for that was found, later, to be the loss in that Province alone.

Yet, as we afterwards came to know, it was not really the fall of snow, tremendous as it had been, which cost the Province nearly all its stock. As I have said, the wind changed to the north-west — the warm quarter — on Sunday night, and it rained heavily as well as blowing half a gale. ... Twenty-four hours of this warm rain and wind was what did all the mischief to the poor sheep. ... Contrary to their custom they had mostly sought refuge beneath the projecting banks of the creeks, and would have been safe enough there if there had not the sudden thaw let the water in on them before they could struggle up, so they were nearly all drowned. ...

During the long bright summer which followed, we used to often ask each other if it could be true that hills had apparently been

Washing day, 1900.

MA_I36195, Museum of New Zealand Te Papa Tongarewa

'Tea in the bush', an illustration from Lady Barker's book *Station Amusements in New Zealand*, which was published in 1873. The image shows a group of settlers sitting in a clearing of bush near a small cabin.

MNZ-0923-1/4-F, Alexander Turnbull Library

levelled and valleys filled up by the heaviest snowstorm ever known. But when we looked at the Ti-ti palms with their topmost leaves gnawed to the stump, we realised that the sheep must have been standing on eight or nine feet of snow to reach them. When the survivors came to be shorn, it was plainly to be seen by the sort of 'nick' in the fleece, where their three weeks' imprisonment had evidently checked the growth of the wool. Many of the hardiest wethers must have been without food for that time, as the pasturage was under either snow or flooded.

AMY PATERSON
THE TARAWERA ERUPTION

The sudden eruption of Mt Tarawera in 1886 both mystified and terrified the occupants of the Rotorua district, many of whom did not know what was going on until hours after the eruption began. At the time of the eruption the Robinson family, including 18-year-old Amy, lived at Awahou, on the northwestern side of Lake Rotorua on the main road to Tauranga. From a distance of about 30 km from the exploding mountain, Amy had a grandstand view of the most spectacular volcanic eruption witnessed by Europeans in New Zealand.

Tarawera Mountain lies to the north-west of Lake Rotorua, and at the foot of this mountain was a small lake called Rotomahana. On each side of this small lake were two terrace formations. On the south side were the white terraces with a boiling cauldron at the top, which at times overflowed and covered this terrace formation with silicated water, covering the whole formation as it flowed down to the bottom into this little lake. Across the lake, where you had to go in a boat for about half a mile, was another terrace formation on a

> **The Mt Tarawera eruption**
>
> The Mt Tarawera eruption lasted six hours. As many as 120 people, almost all of them Maori, lost their lives.

smaller scale, though steeper, which had a pink appearance, and also a boiling cauldron at the top. Like the white terraces they overflowed, filling the large basins with hot water. These Terraces, as well as wonderful, were beautiful, and said to be the largest of their kind in the world.

On the 10th June, 1886, I was living with my parents, some twenty miles as the crow flies from Tarawera. We heard a great noise at 1 a.m., just like a storm brewing, expecting any minute to feel the house shake with the wind; but it kept on and on, and we could not sleep for the noise. We heard our father come into the room next to our bedroom, so we called out, 'What's the matter?' 'Oh!' he said, 'There's an eruption somewhere and I'm going over to see if our old neighbour is safe.'

My mother, sisters and I got up and dressed ourselves, this rumbling noise which was louder than thunder still going on, and the house in a tremble all the time. After the moon had set it was very dark, and on looking out of the door, an awful but grand sight met our gaze; a dark cloud in the western sky; lightning and electricity flashing all through it; red hot stones flying in the air and meeting others coming down, which smashed together and fell into pieces through the dark cloud. The noise was deafening all the time, but there was an awesome feeling about it, and we thought every moment was our last, as even at this time we did not know where it was all happening. However, some of the family went up a hill in front of the house, and through the lightning and electricity flashes they could see Rotorua below it; therefore they concluded that it must be near Rotomahana.

About four o'clock in the morning we heard voices on the road, so we called out 'Who is there?' but the noise was too great for them to hear. Going out to them we found men, women and children, with nothing but their night clothes on and blankets thrown around them. On hearing the roar and noise and seeing flashes of fire (as they thought) they jumped to the conclusion that Sulphur Point, which was a mass of bubbling water and sulphur, was on fire. They jumped out of bed, grabbed a blanket and ran

Buried whare at Te Wairoa after the 1886 eruption of Tarawera.

1/4-002925, photograph taken by the Burton Brothers, 1886, Alexander Turnbull Library

along the street, calling out 'Rotorua is gone and Ohinemutu is going. Put as much land as you can between you and it.' They never stopped to look round till they got to where we were living, some 7 miles from Rotorua, as they were afraid of being caught in it. As it was bitterly cold, we had to take them in and make good fires, and a cup of hot tea. We kept going outside to see the wonderful sight, for fear we missed anything; but we could have enjoyed the awesome sight had we felt we were safe, and not felt that we may be swallowed up at any moment, yet did not know by what.

The night grew darker, so the electricity in the air showed up more plainly every time it flashed through this dark cloud. Still more and more people kept on coming, as we were on the main road, which was in those days the only exit from Rotorua to Tauranga. Eventually we had to put a fire on in the schoolroom (native school) to accommodate all the people. It was well on in the day before the sun got over the dark cloud of mud and ashes from the eruption, and how thankful we were to see the sun, as we began to despair of ever seeing it again.

By this time we were getting all sorts of reports of what was going on, that we did not really know what was happening, as there were no telephones or motor cars in those days. This dark cloud approaching us like a raincloud turned out to be a cloud of sulphurous dust from the eruption, which poured over us for about two hours, but fortunately for us the wind changed and blew it away out to sea in the Bay of Plenty, leaving the whole place covered with a white ash like cement over everything.

When daylight came the people who had arrived first wished they had their clothes on, so some of the men said they would walk back to Rotorua and get some, but were turned back by this sulphurous cloud of steam, choking them. Later on, buggies kept arriving, filled with frightened-looking people, so the men then returned with them to get some clothes. We had to keep these people for a few days till they calmed down, and were able to return to Rotorua.

When we got the real truth of things, we found out that it was an eruption of the Tarawera Mountain which had the whole end blown out, and destroying those beautiful terraces, the beauty of which could never be explained, but one had to see them to know what they were like. I had only been twice over them, as I thought they would always be there to see.

McRae's Hotel, Te Wairoa, after the 1886 eruption of Tarawera.

1/2-020459-F, photograph taken by the Burton Brothers, 1886, Alexander Turnbull Library

WOMEN AT WORK

JANE MARIA RICHMOND
'IN MY ELEMENT'

Jane Maria Richmond emigrated with other members of the extended Richmond and Atkinson families in May 1853, arriving in Auckland on the Sir Edward Paget *and taking the coaster* The Sisters *to New Plymouth. Maria lived there with her mother, also Maria but known as Lely, and various friends and relatives including her brothers James, Henry and William, William's wife Emily (née Atkinson), and Harry and Arthur Atkinson. Arthur and Maria were married in 1854.*

Maria and Arthur lived in Taranaki for the first 14 years of their marriage, before moving to Nelson where they raised four children. Maria died in 1914.

This extract from several of her 'journal letters' records her settling into her adopted home and her feelings of liberation and independence.

Taranaki, 17 Jul 1853

It is now four weeks since I landed from the *Sisters*, and I have found the daily employments of cooking, washing up, sweeping and straightening the house, together with feeble attempts at mending James' and Henry's clothes so completely fill my time that it would have been impossible for me to write a journal letter …

I think as far as I have seen at present colonial life will suit me very well, provided that I have not more than 3 people besides myself to do for, but a larger family unless I had some regular assistance would spoil all my comfort, as I could not keep things in order, nor have time for my needlework, reading, writing or music. We have now 3 cows in milk … making butter up I find very pleasant work. A small family and a nice little dairy I could enjoy, and if the out-door part of the work of the dairy farm, looking after the cows, milking etc., were done by the males, I see no reason why we should be overworked. James has such a thorough horror of servants, that he is delighted to find we have brought none, and I believe there is more comfort without them.

Taranaki, 2 Sep 1853

I am just now a regular maid of all work having to cook and arrange for 13 people … the noise and bustle at meal times is tremendous when all the hungry men turn in from their work and everyone is fetching something and contributing his quota of talk and clatter to the general stock. It is almost too much for Lely at times. She was in first rate spirits but she seems rather inclined to despair of our ever getting set to rights … At present the daily cooking and housework so fill my time that I hardly advance an inch a week towards order.

27 Oct

My own employments consist of a daily succession of cooking bread and butter making, sweeping, cleaning, interspersed now and then with afternoons of ironing and starching, or a faint attempt at gardening, in which department the fowls generally undo in the morning all I have done on the previous afternoon.

8 Nov

It has just occurred to me that I have never distinctly said how I like this country … I may have failed to express the intensity of satisfaction I feel in this new home. I can quite honestly quote old Mr Richardson's 'if you ask me how I like N. Plymouth, I like it, I love it, I thank God for it'. I can say most emphatically that I am disappointed in no single particular, that as far as I can see we acted most wisely in coming here. At the same time I do not think I should dare to advise or persuade anyone to come out. You find people calling the climate execrable because the sun does

> **What does execrable mean?**
>
> To be extremely bad or unpleasant.

not shine perpetually, and because when it does blow or rain it does it in good downright style; you find also people who don't see any beauty in the place because there are no country lanes, hedges, pretty little villages with church spires dotted about. In a perfectly new country you of course miss the finished garden-like appearance that years of cultivation can alone give … but how the absence of such things should blind people to the loveliness before their eyes I cannot understand … I am able to enjoy a great many scenes here that most women never see because few are so fond of scrambling and climbing about as I am.

11 Nov

I am afraid I have the soul of a maid of all work, and whether I shall ever be anything better seems doubtful. Lely seems rather disgusted at seeing me scrub about and look dirty as I do when at dirty work, but I consider myself a much more respectable character than when I was a fine lady, did nothing for anybody but made a great many people do things for me. The worst part of this life is that it makes me fearfully conceited, I am so proud at finding how easy it is to be independent. Lely talks about not being able to bear my being a slave, but I really feel myself less a slave now that I see I can do everything for myself, than I ever did before. When my pantry shelves are scrubbed, and it contains as it will tomorrow afternoon (Saturday) a round of boiled beef, a roast leg of pork, a rhubarb pie, 15 large loaves and 8 pounds of fresh butter ready for Sunday and the bush party, I feel as self-satisfied and proud as a mortal can. A while since I should have thought it necessary to have somebody to prepare all these things for me, now I can do it all myself.

No doubt I am a low unrefined person for deriving satisfaction from such performances, but then as I cannot write a piece of poetry or a tale, not play a piece of music that's worth listening to, nor paint a picture, not sing a song, nor in short do any elegant thing in a satisfactory manner … I am much more in my element here than I ever was before. I am quite certain that the great servant plague in

England must go on increasing till people learn that they are much better and happier in body and mind for not having a separate class to do everything for them [that] they are too stupid, lazy or refined to do for themselves.

13 Nov
At present I cannot see any reason for growing intellectually or morally sleepy in the colonies. I certainly have never felt so wide awake as I have done since I landed in N.Z.; the wonderfulness of the change, the ease and certainty with which one traverses such wastes of water, the suitability of almost all our party to the new situation, the feeling of coming home as it were to a country wanting you, asking for people to enjoy and use it, with a climate to suit you, a beauty to satisfy and delight, and with such capabilities and possibilities for the future, the thinking over all this and a hundred other things of this nature, is enough to make the most sluggish nature 'feel spirited'. Sometimes I am in such a state that I feel convinced nothing short of going up Mt Egmont can properly relieve me and let off the steam; at present I only explode in the baking of 10 loaves or in making up a dozen pounds of butter and an occasional scramble down a gully tearing my clothes nearly to pieces … But imagine a delicate woman coming out, unable to get a servant to stay with her, half killed with work and unable to tear about thro' the bush as I do, what an utterly different feeling she would have; there would be no poetry for her in N.Z., all would be wearisome horrible prose!

Jane Maria Richmond, with sewing basket and needle, and her mother Maria Richmond.

Richmond, Byrne, active 1852. 1/2-079220-F, Alexander Turnbull Library

LIZZIE HEATH
A WIDOW'S OPTIONS

Elizabeth Ovenden came to New Zealand on the Merrington *in 1867 to marry Charles Heath, a marriage arranged by his sister Anne. 'Lizzie' was a widow with an infant son. She married Charles four days after meeting him. After this somewhat hasty start, the marriage was happy enough until Charles' death in 1869, leaving Lizzie pregnant and with two small sons. She was forced to sell his kauri-gum-trading business in the northern Wairoa district of the Kaipara Harbour and run a store to support her growing family. She then married again, this time to the Reverend Moses Breach, and had a fourth child.*

Whakahara, Kaipara, Auckland
Dec. 11 1869

My dearest Anne,
By this time you will have got over the first shock of dear Charles's death, for the first two weeks after I was so exhausted from over fatigue that I could not make myself feel he was gone for ever and that I was again left alone in the world to struggle for a living for my dear children and myself, but 'God's Will be done', I cannot and must not murmur at my loss when I feel so sure it is his gain. It will be an everlasting comfort to me to think I was here to make his last days happy and I pray (little as I was able to do) I was the means

of his preparing to leave this world of sorrow …

You will all be wondering what I am thinking of doing; of course, my mind has thought of many ways to get a living, but I have not been able to talk over the matter to anyone till Mr Gould came and he thinks my plans will answer quite well. I hardly know how to begin to explain matters to you, but I shall do my best. So first of all I must tell you, last summer dear Charles, when in Auckland, made a will in which I am left everything and the lawyer has written to tell me I should have to decide what would be best to be done with the business. Had it been a business a woman could have carried on herself, I would have struggled through it, but it is one entirely with natives, men, and there is so much boating to be done I must have hired labour and taken a partner, then not know the native language,

Tokatoka, c.1882.
Crompton-Smith, Maurice, 1864–1953. A-174-031, Alexander Turnbull Library

I decided [on] having the stock taken, the books made up and having the whole business valued by a disinterested party, for there was Mr Clark who was Charles's partner that was to share half. So after considering well over the advantages and disadvantages, I decided to take £200 and let Mr Clark take everything as it stands. I fear he will be a loser unless the gum trade revives, but I am now freed from all anxiety and I have, with [the] money in [the] house, £300 to put to interest until I settle what to do …

At Tokatoka, not very far from this, we have a large piece of land which is considered to be the best land and position up the river, our gum shed is built on it at the edge of the water (which I ought to tell you is the only piece of private property and a little boat I could call my own before I sold the business), in a few years it will be more valuable as it is at the first township and there are several very large flax companies starting mills up and down the river, and the two public houses there are, no gentleman will go near, but rather get into ever such a poor house. This has been the reason ever since we have been married we have had so many callers, for all say this is the most comfortable English-like home there is in the country, so I have been talking the matter over with Mr Gould as to what he thought of my building a six roomed house on my land at Tokatoka and keeping a private boarding house. Almost every stranger coming up the river has said what a pity someone didn't start one, timber is very dear just now, so that I could not think of buying for a house until the winter …

I must either put the dear little things out to nurse and take a situation, which would be very bad having had a comfortable home or I must struggle and work with my needle and keep them with me. Then living is so much more expensive there and you are so governed by fashion, where here everything is thought fashionable and everyone can wear what they have without being thought peculiar. Then again, this country is so healthy for the dear children and we have two pieces of land that, should

> **What does 'take a situation' mean?**
>
> To take up employment.

they be spared, they can start farming, and here the country is not over crowded with people trying for a living as in England, there is plenty of space and any man can get a living if he is willing to work, and I don't think I shall have much fault to find with mine if I have strength to bring them up as I like. Then again, look at the encouragement I have to get a living here, so many good clothes, and better set up with machinery than anyone in the country. I am sure I ought and do feel most grateful for all the kindness you one and all have shown me, I ought not to flinch from working hard to make the best of what I have and although I may for a year or two have the feeling my little is going out and still less coming in, I feel sure in time I shall be able to make it pay…

Your loving sister, Lizzie.

Mangawhare, Kaipara, Auckland
3 July, 1870

My dearest Sister,
I am thankful I feel better this week, if I can only keep my spirits up I can go through a deal. There is no doubt I must work hard to keep my three children, for it will be years before they can do for themselves. I hope to have strength to teach them to do everything and then they will do far better in this country. The climate is everything that can be desired, but everyone must work hard that has not got an income …

You must all think me very fickle minded, for each letter tells you of some fresh plan I am going to do, but every plan I think of someone advises me to do something else. I must be out of this house by the 1st of January next so you are sure I must decide. Since I wrote to you last, Mr Walton has written to offer his house at Omana (this is where Charles and he used to live when they first came to this country. It is between twenty and thirty miles further up the river), with store and land for a year or so free of all rent, and at the end of that time I can either rent or come to some arrangement about the place, should I find I can make the store answer, or I can build on my own land at Mangakakahi which is just opposite to Omana. I have written to thank him and to accept his offer, but of course I shall not lay a penny out on it, but fence in my orchard and a piece for a garden on my own land, as I shall only have to pull over the river. I intend to creep with regard to a store. I shall first begin by making and selling ready made clothes to the Natives. This, you know, if I can get a sale for, I am sure to manage, but with regard to tea, sugar, flour and such like things I must see how I can get them up to me. No cutter coming from Auckland will bring anything the last twenty miles for less than £[?]. If I have them left at the last calling place I must pay for landing and storage, [and] hire a punt and three men to bring them on. This in fine weather will be the cheapest way, but in winter there is great risk of getting the things damaged …

I have had given me a goat and a pig and I shall buy a cow, for then I can make my own butter and with children plenty of milk is so nice. The goats I can kill — they are a nice small thing for a little family, also pigs. There is plenty of good grass. I have a nice stock of poultry. Indeed, I have a great many things to be thankful for. Not many women left as I am have a better chance of doing [well]. If hard work will ensure me a living, be assured dear friends, I will do my best.

Your ever loving,
E.J. Heath

This pioneer cottage is that of farmer John Lavin. One of the women is likely to be his wife and the child is one of their sons.

Painting by A.J. Cooper, 1861. A-235-012, Alexander Turnbull Library

MARGARET FIDLER
CROQUETTES AND TABLE NAPKINS

Margaret Fidler arrived in New Zealand to join her family in 1877. She had trained in Edinburgh and London's School of Cookery before coming out to New Zealand and becoming a well-known and popular cookery teacher in Dunedin, and later in Palmerston North. The High School referred to is Otago Girls' High School, New Zealand's first public secondary school for girls.

Auld Scotland Hotel Stuart St [Dunedin] July 29th (1877)
My dearest Georg,
I have such a lot of news to tell you that I am sure you will not even guess at. What do you think it is? I know what your thoughts will fly to and you will already be in a fit of jealousy at some unknown young man eh? No it's not that … I'd give you twelve guesses — I've opened a School of Cookery!!! What do you think of that? and I'm getting on splendidly — but I'll just begin at the beginning and tell you all about it. Mrs [?] the lady superintendent of the High School when she knew I had seen those schools at home advocated me starting one here and after thinking over it and summing up what I could do and also what I could manage with

What's a croquette?

A croquette is a small ball of minced meat, vegetables or fish, rolled in breadcrumbs and fried.

> **DUNEDIN SCHOOL OF COOKERY.**
>
> At the opening of the Cookery School in Dunedin, Mr Bathgate, who was in the chair, made the following remarks:— "The introduction of schools of cookery in Great Britain was one of those reforms of modern times which commended itself to every well-wisher of the people generally. He had been expecting for some time past that some of their benevolent and philanthropic ladies would have taken this matter up and have established such classes in Dunedin. He was glad to see that through the private enterprise of Miss Fidler, such a school was at length established. In his sad professional experience, he had known numberless cases in which households would have been kept together if the "better half" had been a better cook. There was an old saying that the surest way to a man's affections was through his stomach. He did not know whether that was true or not, but in Parliamentary affairs the votes of doubtful members were generally sought to be obtained by inviting them to dinner. Those who had been started in life for any length of time knew that their comfort, to a great extent, depened upon the domestic servants, and if they were able to introduce thoroughly equipped cooks, he thought he was only expressing the opinion of everyone present when he said that great advantages would follow. One lesson in each course would be devoted to sick-room cookery—a class of cooking which required special attention. It, therefore, was a matter of congratulation that some attention was to be given to that subject. He wished all the ladies present to banish from their minds the idea that because they belonged to the fair sex, therefore they had an intuitive knowledge of cookery. An apprenticeship must be served to that as well as anything else, so he hoped that these classes would be largely attended by young ladies, and, by adding this qualification to their existing charms, they would improve their chances in the matrimonial market.

The opening of Margaret Fidler's cookery school merited an article in the *Grey River Argus* newspaper.

Papers Past, National Library of New Zealand, *Grey River Argus*, Volume XXI, Issue 2791, 24 July 1877

practice I at last consented not to have one in connection with the school but on my own responsibility for if I had failed I would rather have borne it myself than had anyone else do it. Well Jack is our right-hand man in all things and he helped me so much in this if it had not been for him the project would have ended in mere words for there was so much to do in the way of getting advertisements and prospectuses printed and a great many general things to manage that I knew very little about. Mrs [?] introduced me to Professor [?] who came from home two years ago to be the Professor of Anatomy at the University — he had seen the Schools at Home and readily undertook to give an opening lecture. I've been figuring largely in the papers dear and I'll send you their opinion as it won't be one-sided as I might be.

I commenced this undertaking in fear and trembling and until it was really commenced I was quite miserable and until the last moment I was sure I would break down but you know in former cases I have been the same, and when I am brought to the proper pitch I can go through anything and so it was in this case. At the lecture Professor [?] was anxious that I should show how the classes were conducted so I had the ingredients prepared and made some croquettes, folded a table napkin in a pretty shape and ornamented them with chillies and parsley. I felt as much possessed as a duchess … I wore my black silk and green felt bonnet done up with ecru terry and silk at the lecture, but now you may imagine me figuring [?] two hours five days a week on a small platform dressed in a grey princess dress, muslin apron with bib, muslin sleeves …

I managed to get a nice sized hall and the only suitable stove (gas) in Dunedin. I have all the necessary requirements for cooking ranged on two shelves behind me and a servant to do the washing up and handing me things. I have a large class of ladies both married and single in the afternoon 50 there are and this I call my special class and I enjoy it so much. My pupils are considered the elite of the town [and] are appreciative of the good things I make. I find this class will quite cover all expenses and as I intend to respect the course of twelve lessons before closing for the winter I'll perhaps be in possession of a small fortune that may one day bring me home to you my darling. I have got six of my special class and six of my evening classes over and I am going to send you the list of what I have done when the twelve lessons are over. The report in the [Otago Daily] Times I have sent was written after the sixth lessons in both classes were concluded …

If you can give me any useful hints from Williamson I know you will — I have got his cooking book but seeing his receipts practically done is better … The paper said I had four subjects at a lesson but I always manage six and sometimes seven — I was just preparing for this when I wrote you last but I thought I would not tell you until everything was in working order and I could enter into particulars. I am going to finish for tonight so goodnight my darling.

Otago Girls' High School was New Zealand's first public secondary school for girls.

'Girls new High School, Dunedin, 1910', photograph by Muir & Moodie Studio. LS.003590, Museum of New Zealand Te Papa Tongarewa

ELLEN WILSON & OTHER WITNESSES
THE 'SWEATING COMMISSION'

The number and size of factories in New Zealand grew rapidly during the late nineteenth century, as the population expanded and export industries developed. The clothing industry in particular experienced great growth, and it employed many women, who had the necessary skills and could be paid less than men. In 1888, a Presbyterian minister, the Reverend Rutherford Waddell, spoke out against abuses in the clothing trade in Dunedin, claiming that the practice of 'sweating' — employees working long hours for very low pay — was being carried out. Many people were disturbed by the allegations, because they considered New Zealand free of such 'social evils' that plagued industrialised England.

In 1889 a Royal Commission was appointed 'to inquire into the relations between employers and employees in the colony'. The 'Sweating Commission', as it was known, heard evidence from workers around the country and found that not only women but children too were working under undesirable conditions. The Liberal Government, which came to power in 1891, passed legislation to control working conditions in factories and shops, and set up the Department of Labour to police these laws.

The evidence of the following women — the majority anonymous to protect their employment — speaks for itself. It is worth noting that a male labourer of the time would have earned around 6 shillings per day.

The extracts reproduced here are taken from the original document presented to Parliament.

Ellen Wilson examined

I am a shirt finisher, and work at —. Things are very different from what they were twelve months since, when the agitation commenced.

There is very little to complain of now. Sixteen months since it was hardly possible to earn a living. The best week I had then, working hard, was 10s. 6d; that was working from 9 in the morning till 11 at night, with no hours off for meals. I got about ten minutes for dinner, and when I got home at night I used to take a short time to do a little extra cooking; but could scarcely take time to get my meals. I can now make 12s. or 13s. a week; and a good finisher would make 18s. a week inside the eight hours per day. I can make 12s. per week now, working eight hours a day, whereas before it took me fourteen hours to make 1s. 10 and a half d.

The [Tailoresses] Union has been a great boon to us. I would not for anything it was dissolved, because it has done away with taking work home at night. There are some who say they would rather take work home; but they have sisters, cousins or women to help them. When you take home eight or nine shirts amongst four people that is nothing , but if you take half a dozen, and have to put in every stitch yourself it is a different matter …

The long hours affected my health. I sat up late, and in the morning I really could not get up. This made it later going to work, and I never felt refreshed.

I do not complain of the wages now at all. Some make more than I do; but I am always content with 12s. a week. I know of some making 16s. and 18s. a week, and I have heard of one making 22s. in another place, but that depends a good deal on the kind of work done.

I think I could just live on from 8s. to 9s. a week; but I am a small

Part of the opening page of the official report of the Sweating Commission.

Sweating Commission. (Report of the Royal Commission appointed to inquire into certain relations between the employers of certain kinds of labour and the persons employed therein.) Appendix to the Journals of the House of Representatives, 1890, Session I, H-05

Workers inside the Kaiapoi Woollen Company factory, c.1910.

1/1-007898-G, Alexander Turnbull Library, Wellington, New Zealand

eater. I can live and clothe myself on 12s. a week.

I think girls like their evenings to themselves, and that they do not like [domestic] situations. I know big strong girls at this work, and I have often wondered why they should work for 12s. a week. I would not do so if I had been strong enough to go into service. I could not do that class of work or I would not have gone to the finishing, but would have gone to a situation. I have been in several situations, but had to give them up as I was not strong enough for the work.

If I were laid up by illness I should have to go to the hospital, as I could not save anything from my earnings.

Miss D.E. examined

I am a dressmaker now, but it was in relation to domestic servants that I wished to make a complaint. When in that capacity I used to work sixteen hours a day. I was allowed one night a week off, and regularly every other Saturday and Sunday night. My wages were 9s. a week. I commenced work at 6.30 a.m. and left off at 11 p.m., and was working all the time, either ironing or sewing or something after the ordinary housework was done. I was well cared for, but I objected to the long hours. I consider the mistress of the house should assist, and so lighten the work. I have been in service at four different houses, and three of the mistresses were tyrants. I consider the hours of domestic servants should be regulated the same as those of lumpers on the wharf. Mistresses should be compelled to keep more than one servant when necessary. I do not find fault with the wages, but I think the work should be reduced so as to make the hours less.

I am only just starting dressmaking, and am kept by my mother. I went to another place as an improver at 8s. a week, and am there now. I am not yet a competent hand, but my brother is going to pay a premium for me to learn the trade.

It is the hard work and not pride which causes

The alternative to factory work for many women was domestic service, where hours were longer and conditions arguably worse.

Schourup, Peter, 1837–1887. PA2-2083, Alexander Turnbull Library

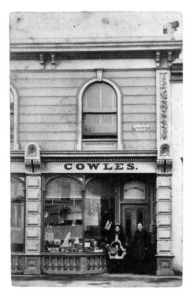

Some women ran their own businesses. This is Mrs Cowles' toy shop on Lambton Quay in Wellington, around 1880.

1/2-056053-F, Alexander Turnbull Library, Wellington, New Zealand

girls to give up being domestic servants and go into factories. I would sooner be a servant if I could get a good mistress.

Miss Y. examined

I am employed at Clarke's steam laundry in the North-east Valley.

We have pretty long hours — from 8 a.m. to 6 p.m., with only half an hour for dinner. The hours are the same on Saturdays.

We are at piecework, and prices vary. I make more sometimes than at other times —about £1 a week.

The room we work in is pretty warm. The stoves for irons are going all day.

I am employed ironing shirts.

About twenty-five women are employed in the laundry, and there is an engineer and a lad who drives the express also employed there.

We have no complaint to make, except we want an hour for dinner. We need the rest in the middle of the day.

We do not get any holidays excepting Christmas Day, and sometimes New Years Day.

I have been ill, and most of the others get ill after a time: I think it is from the heat and the standing …

There are young girls working there. Two of them are about twelve years of age, and the next would be sixteen years old. All work the same hours.

ACKNOWLEDGEMENTS AND SOURCES

The stories that appear in this collection were originally published in two selections, *The Adventures of Pioneer Women in New Zealand* (Bush Press, 1992) and *The Lives of Pioneer Women in New Zealand* (Bush Press, 1993). Some stories have been abridged for this editon.

Here is a list of published sources from which material has been drawn:

Barker, Lady Mary Anne, *Colonial Memories*, Smith, Elder & Co., London, 1904.

Godley, Charlotte, *Letters from Early New Zealand by Charlotte Godley 1850–1853*, edited, with notes by John R. Godley, printed for private circulation only 1936; Canterbury Centennial Edition 1951, Whitcombe and Tombs Ltd, Christchurch, 1951.

'Hopeful', *Taken In; Being a Sketch of New Zealand Life*, W. H. Allen & Co., London, 1887.

Minutes of Evidence Taken before the Royal Commission Appointed to Inquire into the Relations between Employers and Employed in the Colony, Appendices to the Journal of the House of Representatives, 1890, H-5.

The following authors are quoted from diaries, letters and reminiscences held by the Alexander Turnbull Library, and are reproduced with their permission.

Adams, Eleanor: Adams, Eleanor, 1876–1958: The Milford Track, MS-Papers-3542.

Adams, Martha: Adams, Martha, 1815–1906, Papers, qMS-0026.

Chevalier, Caroline: Chevalier, Caroline 1832–1836?–1917: Reminiscences of a journey across the South Island, qMS-0438.

Chitty, Alicia: Chitty, Alicia Wilhemina, b. 1858, Autobiographical sketch, qMS-0446.

Coote, Rhoda: Coote, Rhoda Carleton (Holmes), 1822–1892: Papers, MS-Papers-1248.

Fidler, Margaret: Letters c.1877, MS-Papers 3484.

Findlayson, Jane: Diary 1876–77, MS-Papers 1678.

Heath, Lizzie: Heath, Charles, d 1869: Letters from Charles Heath of Kaipara and his wife, Lizzie to and from their family in England, qMS-0939.

Higgins, Sarah: Higgins, Sarah, 1830–1923: Autobiography, MS-Papers-3894.

Holman, Elizabeth: Holman, Elizabeth A. 1824–1917: Reminiscences, qMS-0993.

Langford, Harriet: Langford, Harriet, 1818-1898 : Our early days in New Zealand/written by Mrs John Alfred Langford, MS-Papers-3411.

Mathew, Sarah Louisa: Mathew, Sarah Louisa 1805–1890: Extracts from diary (autobiography) of Mrs Felton Mathew, qMS-1350.

Paterson, Amy: Paterson, Amy (Robinson) : A contemporary account of the Tarawera eruption, MS-1764.

Richmond, Jane Maria: Family correspondence [WGa Vol 39], MSX-3020.

INDEX

A
Adams, Eleanor 55–59
Adams, Martha 33–38
Adams, William 33–38
Arthur's Pass 50
Auckland 46, 62, 64, 66, 82, 87, 90
Aurora 24

B
Barker, Lady Mary Anne 71–75
Bolton 29, 32
Broome, Frederick Napier 71, 73
Buenos Aires 14
Butter making 40–41, 82–85, 90

C
Canterbury 11, 50, 67, 70–75
Cape of Good Hope 14–15
Chitty, Alicia Wilhemina 39–43
Chitty, Walter 39, 42
Chevalier, Caroline 50–54
Chevalier, Nicholas 50–54
Christchurch 8, 71–72
Clothing factories 94–96
Coote, Rhoda 67–70
Coronilla 39, 43
County Tipperary, Ireland 39

D
Deal, England 39
De Vere Hunt, Mathew 39, 43
Dunedin 11, 16, 59, 91–93
D'Urville Island 24

E
Earthquakes 67–70
Eden 33
Edinburgh 91

F
Fidler, Margaret 91–93

Findlayson, Jane 16–21
Flowers 47, 58–59

G
Godley, Charlotte 11–15
Gold 48, 50–52, 62
Greenock, Scotland 16

H
Hamilton East 39, 42–43
Heath, Charles 86–89
Heath, Lizzie 86–90
Heke, Hone 62–64, 66
Higgins, Sarah 29–32
Higgins, Sidney 29, 31
Hokitika 51
Holman, Elizabeth 62–66
Holman, Henry 62–66
Horses 17, 32–35, 39, 42, 46, 51–54, 59, 68, 73
Hukanui 39
Hutt River 26

K
Kaiapoi Woollen Company 96
Kaipara 86–90
Kauri 62, 86
Kawau Island 65
Kent, England 29

L
Lady Nugent 11–15
Langford, James Alfred 24, 27
Langford, Harriet 24–28
London, England 46, 91

M
Marlborough 33
Mathew, Felton 46, 49
Mathew, Sarah 46–49
Merrington 86
Milford Track 55–59
Milking 31, 41, 82–83, 90
Mt Tarawera 76–79

N
Nelson 29–33, 35, 82
New Plymouth 82–85

Northland 46, 62

O
Oamaru 16–21
Otago Girls' High School 91–93
Otago Harbour 14–15

P
Palmerston North 91
Paterson, Amy 76–79
Petone 25–26
Port Chalmers 14–15, 21
Port Nicholson 24
Plymouth, England 11, 14

R
Rangitoto 46
Rats 19, 54, 57
Richmond, Jane Maria 82–85
Rotorua 76–79
Russell (Kororareka) 62–64

S
Sheep 33–36, 41–42, 59, 71, 74–75
Sir Edward Paget 82
Snares Island 14
Snow 32, 71–75
Stewart Island 14–15
Suffragette Petition 26
Sweating Commission 95–95
Sydney, Australia 46

T
Tasmania 46
The Sisters 82
Tokatoka 87–88

W
Wairau 33–38
Wellington 11, 24–25, 67–70
Westland 50
Whangarei 62, 64, 66
Wilson, Ellen 94–96